CARB & CALORIE COUNTER

M000283310

- ★ Over 1,700 foods
- ★ A visual way to count your carbs, calories, protein, fat, saturated fat, fibre & 5-a-day
- ★ Also available as a pocket version

FLASHCARDS

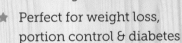

- ★ 54 cards in each pack
- ★ Range of popular food & drinks
- ★ Perfect for teaching & learning

MOBILE APP

Available for iPhone & Android

- ★ Over 3,500 photos, including branded foods
- ★ Perfect for weight loss, portion control & diabetes
- ★ The ultimate portable calorie counter!

PLUS...
FREE HEALTH RESOURCES

FREE!

- ★ Register for FREE access to 50 PDF resources
- ★ www.carbsandcals.com/register

Visit www.carbsandcals.com

Carbs & Cals SOUPS

80 healthy soup recipes plus 275 ingredient photos to create your own!

1ST EDITION

First published in Great Britain in 2016
by Chello Publishing Limited

Registered Company Number 7237986

www.chellopublishing.co.uk | info@chellopublishing.co.uk

Copyright © Chello Publishing Limited 2016

With special thanks to: Fran Turner, George Malache, Gian Mizzi, Justine Rose, Maxine Gregory, Simon Callaghan, Victoria Francis, Warren Thorpe, and Yoshi Balolia

The information contained in this book is not a substitute for medical or other professional guidance. Please consult your GP before making any alterations to medications or changing medical treatment. Although all reasonable care has been taken in the writing of this book, the authors and publisher are not responsible for any specific health needs; they do not accept any legal responsibility or liability for any personal injury or other consequences, damage or loss arising from any use of information and advice contained within this book.

The authors have asserted their moral rights.

ISBN: 978-1-908261-21-2 Printed in Malta 1116

Authors	Chris Cheyette BSc (Hons) MSc RD
	Yello Balolia BA (Hons)
Recipes by	Chris Cheyette BSc (Hons) MSc RD
	Victoria Francis BSc (Hons) RD
Photography	Simon Callaghan & Francesca Turner
Design Concept	George F Malache
Graphic Design	Maxine Gregory BA (Hons)
Additional Layout	Yello Balolia BA (Hons)
Introduction Text	Victoria Francis BSc (Hons) RD

For more information, please visit:

www.carbsandcals.com

Contents

Introduction

Did your grandma ever make you a bowl of chicken soup to feed your cold, soothe your cough and stifle your sniffles? A steaming bowl of soup can be nourishing and comforting. It makes you feel a little less sorry for yourself when under the weather, or when you've trudged home in the bitter wind and rain. So, as the days get colder, the nights draw in and when a bowl of crunchy salad just isn't tempting, it can only mean one thing... it's soup season!

Soups can be a quick and simple light meal option, a meal addition, a great starter choice when eating out or a quick, warming snack – a cup of soup and away you go!

Of course, not all soups are for the autumn and winter months. Let's not forget the lovely chilled soups such as gazpacho that can be cooling and refreshing on a warm summer's day.

This is just the beginning of the versatility of soups; the great thing about them is that you can freestyle your methods and not go too far wrong. As long as you have a few of the essential recipe components, you can experiment with new flavours and ingredients. Soups are a great vehicle for veggies - ones that you don't know what to do with, have an abundance of, or are looking a little tired and coming to the end of their days. They're also a covert way to get extra vegetables into your loved ones!

For example, if you are struggling to think how you can add more pulses and legumes to your diet, throw a handful of lentils into your soup to thicken and add extra goodness. This simple addition will boost your intake of fibre, protein and iron.

As well as the variety of nutrients that can be packed into a serving, soups are often low in calories so a great meal choice when trying to watch your intake. The bulk from the liquid, vegetables and fibre will keep you feeling full and satisfied.

If you want to improve your diet, boost your fibre intake or lose weight, then soups are a must. This book will show you how soups can be incorporated into all healthy eating plans. Using evidence-based nutrition facts and a wide variety of recipes, you will be helped to achieve your dietary goals and tickle your taste buds at the same time.

Still need convincing? They are "souper" easy to make, often using only one pan. You can even put everything in the slow cooker before you start work in the morning, to be ready for your evening meal. Made too much? Simply freeze for a day when the cupboards are empty and your energy levels are low.

Health benefits of soups

Homemade soups are preferable to pre-made ones, as you control what (and how much) is put in! Many pre-made soups contain large amounts of salt and tend to be low in protein but high in carbs, due to their potato base.

Reach your 5-a-day... soups are a vehicle for veggies!

There is an abundance of scientific evidence supporting the role of fruit and vegetables in our diet to protect against ill health and diseases such as cancer.

The current advice is to consume 400g (5 portions) of fruit and vegetables per day. It is important to note that this amount is only the minimum. Research shows that a third of adults do not meet these recommendations, so slurp up your soup to help reach your 5-a-day!

Page
82

5
5-a-day

Almond & Greens Soup

1
5-a-day

½
5-a-day

Sweetcorn
40g

Cherry Tomatoes
80g

Page
83

5
5-a-day

Sweet Gingered
Vegetable
Soup

Each of the following counts
as 1 portion of your 5-a-day:

★ 80g fresh, frozen or tinned
fruit or vegetables
★ 30g dried fruit
★ 150ml pure, unsweetened
fruit or vegetable juice
★ 80g beans and pulses

Using a rainbow of vegetables
(and even fruit) in your soups will
provide you with a wide variety
of nutrients (including vitamins
A and C), fibre, phytonutrients
and antioxidants, all of which will
nourish your body and reduce
the risk of health problems.

Ten of the soup recipes in this
book contain all 5 of your 5-a-day.

Looking for another way to get your 5-a-day?

Check out our salads
book for more ideas
on tasty and inventive
ways to reach your
5-a-day in one hit!

6
5-a-day

Reduce your calories with little effort

Soups can be a great tool when trying to lose weight. Vegetables pack a punch in that they are low in calories but a great source of fibre, vitamins and minerals. The combination of liquid and veg adds bulk and keeps you feeling full with fewer calories. Adding protein further keeps you feeling satisfied and less likely to nibble on the "naughties". In one study, a group of volunteers reduced their total lunch calories by an average of 20 percent when they began the meal with low-calorie vegetable soup before eating pasta.

115 Cals

Page **46**

Tomato & Basil Soup

Red Onions 20g

7 Cals

King Prawns 70g

48 Cals

Mushrooms 80g

6 Cals

Spinach 20g

5 Cals

Carrots 40g

14 Cals

Increase your fibre intake

Vegetables are the predominant base ingredients for a soup and are a great source of fibre. The link between total fibre intake and lowered risk of heart disease, bowel cancer and type 2 diabetes has led the Scientific Advisory Committee on Nutrition to revise and update fibre recommendations to 30g per day for adults (the current average intake is 18g per day). Adding pulses and grains to your soup will further boost the soluble fibre content, which is known to help control blood glucose levels, lower cholesterol levels, slow down digestion and keep you feeling full.

13g
Fibre

Black Eye
Avocado
Soup

Page
90

5g
Fibre

Cannellini
Beans 80g

3g
Fibre

Lentils 80g

Pump up your plant-based proteins

When people think of protein, chicken, meat and fish often most quickly spring to mind. However, due to the link between processed meat and an increased risk of bowel cancer, the Department of Health has advised people to limit the amount of red and processed meat to 70g per day (or 500g per week). For health and environmental reasons, there is a big move towards using more plant-based proteins like beans, pulses, nuts, tofu and grains such as quinoa. Soups are a great way to introduce these foods into your diet, e.g. quinoa can be added to soup to thicken it or toasted nuts can be a simple, nutritious garnish.

Page 103
21g Protein

Moroccan Harira Chickpea Soup

Tofu 80g

19g Protein

Soya Beans 80g

11g Protein

Curb your cooking costs

As already mentioned, soups are a great way to minimise waste, as you can throw in any leftovers lurking at the back of your fridge. Even if it has been a while since your last shop, by using a few basic store cupboard ingredients such as stock, herbs & spices, vegetables and tinned pulses, you can quickly cook-up a bowl of soup. It can also be a cheap option if you are feeding the masses – chopped carrots, dried lentils, stock, spices and a few other ingredients are all you need for a pot of Spicy Carrot & Lentil soup. Cheap, simple and nutritious!

Spicy Carrot
& Lentil
Soup

Page
53

Basil
6 leaves

Butter
Beans
80g

Ingredient Health Benefits

Apple
Rich in cancer-fighting antioxidants

Beetroot
Source of folic acid, key nutrient if planning a pregnancy

Cabbage
High in both fibre and water, cabbage can help prevent constipation

Pak Choi
Low in calories and fat, so great if you are trying to lose weigh

Spinach
Rich in magnesium, which helps to calm the body and relax muscles

Tomato
Contains lycopene, an antioxidant known to protect against heart disease

Avocado
Contains vitamin E, to help keep your skin healthy

Butternut Squash
Protects your immune system, due to its vitamin A content

Ginger
Known to alleviate discomfort and pain in the stomach

Parsnip
Source of iron, important for preventing anaemia

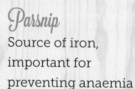

Sweet Potato
Fibre-rich and a source of slow releasing energy

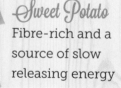

Yellow Pepper
High in beta-carotene (which makes vitamin A) to avoid an itchy scalp and dry hair

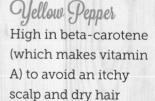

Chickpeas
Low in fat and high in fibre, ideal for weight loss plans

Lentils
Rich in iron, needed to carry oxygen around to your cells and prevent anaemia

Pearl Barley
High in fibre and a source of slow releasing energy

Quinoa
Excellent source of B vitamins, for a healthy nervous system

Egg
Rich in vitamin D, important for healthy bones

Mussels
Good source of zinc, an essential nutrient for optimum fertility

Tofu
Contains all 8 essential amino acids, used by the body to build proteins

Salmon
Protective against heart disease due to its high content of omega-3 fatty acids

Almonds
High in heart-healthy unsaturated fats

Hazelnuts
Fibre-rich, for a healthy digestive system

Pumpkin Seeds
An excellent source of magnesium, for strong bones and muscle relaxation

Walnuts
Anti-inflammatory, so great for those suffering with joint pain and arthritis

Soups as part of your diet plan

What is a healthy, balanced diet and how can soups be included?

The health benefits of a balanced diet include a better ability to manage weight, as well as a reduced risk of long term conditions such as cancer and heart disease. But what constitutes a healthy diet? It should contain appropriate proportions of a variety of nutrient-rich foods, such as:

★ Vegetables and fruit for antioxidants, vitamins and minerals

★ Dairy foods, such as milk and yogurt, for calcium

★ Wholegrain carbohydrates, such as oats, brown rice and puy lentils, for B vitamins and fibre

★ Meat, fish, nuts, eggs and quinoa for good quality protein

★ Oily fish and nuts for omega-3 oils

Soups definitely have their place on a healthy, balanced dietary plan thanks to the nutrient-rich foods they commonly contain. Whatever your health goal, the key to achieving success is finding a sustainable approach that works for you and your lifestyle. Soups can be incorporated into a variety of meal plans.

5:2 diet

The 5:2 approach involves eating a healthy, balanced diet for 5 days and fasting on the remaining 2 days each week (500 calories for women and 600 calories for men), achieving an overall 25% reduction in calories. For many, this may feel unachievable without feeling constantly hungry. Fibre and protein are known to keep us feeling full, so to get through the day your dishes need to be rich in these nutrients to help you feel satisfied. Soups are a great way to keep the calories down, but your protein and fibre intake high.

Our creamy Broccoli & Fennel soup contains 8g protein but only 145 calories, making it a perfect lunchtime choice. Or choose the White Bean & Kale soup for dinner, which contains 225 calories, 14g fibre (nearly half of your daily target) and 4 of your 5-a-day, even on a fast day! Please see page 23 about how to incorporate soups into your 5:2 diet plan.

Broccoli & Fennel Soup

145 Cals

Page **30**

5:2 Diet Photos
To buy your copy, visit:
www.carbsandcals.com/5-2

Very low-calorie diet

Recent evidence has shown that a very low-calorie diet of under 800 calories per day for two months causes significant weight loss, and can reverse the insulin resistance that is common in type 2 diabetes or those diagnosed with pre-diabetes. Each mouthful has to pack a nutritious punch and fill you up, so turning to low-calorie vegetables and plant-based proteins seems the obvious choice.

See our Low-Calorie Soups chapter (pages 38 - 47) for 10 recipes with 120 calories or less!

95 Cals

Carrot & Orange Soup

Page 39

Page 44

Leek & Pea Soup

115 Cals

Low-carb diets

Low-carbohydrate diets are popular among people with abnormally high blood glucose levels, as carbohydrate is the key nutrient that affects the rise in blood glucose. Vegetables are naturally low in carbs, so make the ideal choice when trying to keep carb intake low.

There are 30 soups in this book containing under 20g carbs.

High-protein diets

Foods high in protein help you feel fuller for longer, so increasing the proportion of protein in the diet can help to satisfy your hunger with minimal impact on blood glucose levels.

Spring Chicken soup has 44g protein in only 295 calories, making it a great lunch choice.

High-fibre diets

The average UK adult currently consumes 18g fibre per day, so for many it may seem a tall order to reach the new recommendation of 30g per day.

Choosing our Bean & Barley soup will provide a whopping 15g of fibre (50% of your daily target) for only 305 calories!

Creamy Brie & Mushroom Soup

8g Carbs

Page 35

Spring Chicken Soup

44g Protein

Page 98

Bean & Barley Soup

15g Fibre

Page 94

Soups for people with diabetes

Diabetes is a condition in which glucose levels in the blood are too high because the body cannot process the glucose properly. The two main types of diabetes are type 1 and type 2.

Type 1 diabetes develops because the immune system attacks and destroys the cells that produce insulin, which regulates glucose in the blood. This leads to high blood glucose levels. It is treated through the administration of insulin via injection or pump. For people with type 1 diabetes who adjust their insulin dose according to their carbohydrate intake, soups can be included in their diet as long as the carbohydrate content is calculated and matched with quick acting insulin.

PLEASE NOTE: The carbs displayed with each soup are the total carbs from all ingredients, including vegetables, pulses and grains. When calculating an insulin dose, some will need to make a note of the source of carbohydrate and subtract the carb content of certain foods (such as vegetables and pulses). For further guidance on how to count the carbs in a soup and match with quick acting insulin, speak with your diabetes dietitian or nurse specialist.

Type 2 diabetes develops when the pancreas does not produce enough insulin, or the body is unable to use the insulin effectively (known as insulin resistance). Type 2 diabetes can primarily be treated with a healthy diet and lifestyle change, such as increased physical activity. However, it is a progressive condition and many people may need to commence medication at some point, in order to control their blood glucose levels.

For most people with type 2 diabetes, weight loss is the primary goal to reduce insulin resistance and improve insulin sensitivity. Emerging evidence supports the short-term use of a very low-calorie diet (800 calories per day) to reverse insulin resistance and type 2 diabetes in some people. Because of their high fibre content and low energy density, soups play a pivotal role in such weight loss diets.

If you have diabetes and are taking medication (including insulin), speak with your healthcare professional for guidance on losing weight and how to include soups in your daily diet.

How to use this book

This book includes 80 carefully created soup recipes, divided into the following sections:

Low-Carb Pages **28 - 37**

8g Carbs

Low-Calorie Pages **38 - 47**

110 Cals

General Recipes Pages **48 - 77**

5 5-a-day

275 Cals

5-a-day Pages **78 - 87**

13g Fibre

High-Fibre Pages **88 - 97**

43g Protein

High-Protein Pages **98 - 107**

Within each section, the soups are listed in calorie order, starting with the lowest calorie recipe. For each soup, the nutritional information for the following nutrients are clearly displayed in colour-coded circles:

Cals   5-a-day   Fibre   SatFat   Fat   Protein   Carbs

Simply browse the variety of recipes and select ones that meet your dietary goal.

Avocado
70g

A few things to note:

★ **All recipes in this book will make 1 portion.** If you wish to make a dish for 2 people, simply double the recipe.

★ The recipes use average/medium sizes of vegetables and fruit, and weights shown are for the edible part (after being peeled or stoned), unless otherwise stated.

★ Some recipes use a handy measure (e.g. handful of kale) instead of a specific weight. Should you wish to know the exact weights, simply find that portion in the ingredients section. For example, the Kale & Greens soup on page 41 uses 2 handfuls of kale. Looking at kale on page 137, you will see that 2 handfuls weigh 40g.

Kale & Greens
Soup

110
Cals

Page
41

1g
Protein

1g
Fat

Kale
40g, 2 handfuls

2g
Fibre

1g
Carbs

13
Cals

½
5-a-day

★ The recipes often do not include salt & pepper, as adding seasoning is down to personal taste. Such addition will not affect the calorie content.

★ The recipes use a mix of uncooked and cooked weights for rice, pasta, couscous, quinoa and pearl barley. The table below outlines the simple conversion for uncooked and cooked weights, although please bear in mind that the longer you cook your pasta and rice, the more water it absorbs, which will affect the final weight of the cooked product.

	Uncooked Weight	Cooked Weight
Couscous	35g	80g
Dried Pasta	45g	100g
Pearl Barley	25g	80g
Quinoa	30g	80g
Rice	35g	100g

Minestrone with Basil Pesto Soup

325 Cals

Page 80

White Fusilli Pasta 100g

Pearl Barley 80g

Creating your own recipes

The potential soup combinations are endless, so why not get creative?
Try making up your own using the list of ingredients at the back
of this book (pages 108 to 155). The nutritional content of each
individual ingredient is shown, giving you the flexibility to create
soup recipes to meet your own personal dietary goal. It's worth
writing down the details of your creations so you have a record of
nutritional information and can make the recipe again in future.

Mixed Beans (tinned)
80g, drained

5g Protein
1g Fat
5g Fibre
10g Carbs
78 Cals
1 5-a-day

Butternut Squash
80g

1g Protein
0g Fat
2g Fibre
7g Carbs
29 Cals
1 5-a-day

Courgette
80g, 1/3 medium

1g Protein
0g Fat
1g Fibre
1g Carbs
14 Cals
1 5-a-day

My soup

Mixed Beans 80g (78 cals)

Butternut
Squash 80g   (29 cals)

Courgette 80g   (14 cals)

TOTAL = 121 cals

Making a 5:2 diet meal plan

The 5:2 diet works by fasting on 2 days of the week and eating a healthy, balanced diet on the remaining 5 days. This 25% reduction in calories has proven to be an effective weight loss method for many people.

Here is an example of how to include soup into your fasting day:

1. Decide how you would like to split your calorie allowance for the day. For example, your 500 calories could be made up of two or three meals spread throughout the day:
   - ★ 100 cals for breakfast
   - ★ 100 cals for lunch
   - ★ 300 cals for dinner

2. Browse this book and decide which soup meets your dietary needs. If you normally get hungry mid afternoon, you may wish to choose a high-protein soup for lunch, to keep you feeling full for the rest of the afternoon. Alternatively, you may wish to choose a light soup at lunch to allow for a larger evening meal.

3. Use this book alongside our Smoothies, Salads or 5:2 Diet Photos book, to make your fasting days feel like a feast, not a famine!

Daily meal plan:

Breakfast:

100 Cals

3 5-a-day

Orangetastic Smoothie

Lunch:

95 Cals

2½ 5-a-day

Herbed Triple Tomato Salad

Dinner:

315 Cals

1½ 5-a-day

Page **65**

Chicken Pho Soup

Total: **510** Cals **7** 5-a-day

Producing a meal plan for a 1500 calorie diet

Low-calorie diets, defined as 800-1600 calories per day, can be achieved through careful selection of foods and control of portion sizes. Following a 1500 calorie diet plan can help you lose around ½kg (1lb) a week (more if you have lots to lose), without feeling you are depriving yourself of everything.

Soups are a great way to ensure you meet your nutrient needs whilst limiting your calorie intake.

Daily meal plan:

Breakfast:

Chia Seed
Breakfast Pot

50 Cals

1 5-a-day

Orange Juice
150ml

235 Cals

½ 5-a-day

Snack:

Large
Banana

104 Cals

1 5-a-day

For information on weight loss and working out your calorie target, visit:

www.carbsandcals.com/BMI

Lunch:

Parsnip & Hazelnuts Soup

360 Cals

2 5-a-day

Page 69

147 Cals

Wholemeal Pitta

Snack:

116 Cals

Cappuccino Medium

Dinner:

Chicken & Cashew Stir-fry

360 Cals

3 5-a-day

Cooked Rice 100g

117 Cals

Total: 1489 Cals 7½ 5-a-day

Buying ingredients

★ Where possible, use wholegrain pasta and rice to boost fibre content.

★ Always use fresh, ripe fruit and vegetables.

★ Try to use organic produce where possible.

★ To keep the cost down, choose vegetables and fruit that are in season. Alternatively, you can replace one vegetable with another that is in season, but be mindful that this may change the nutritional content.

★ Use olive oil for cooking.

★ The thickness of shop-bought tahini paste can vary, so you may wish to add more water to achieve the desired consistency.

★ A great way to add variety to your diet and ensure you always have your soup ingredients to hand is to order a fruit and vegetable box. Each delivery is different, so you never know what soup recipe will be on the menu!

To see our recommended veg box companies, please visit:
www.carbsandcals.com/vegbox

Cooking Glossary

Drizzle: Pour a small amount of liquid on or into soup.

Flake: Use a fork, or hand, to break cooked fish into smaller pieces and to check if the fish is cooked. If cooked, the fish flesh should fall away easily.

Matchstick: Cut into thin strips.

Mince: Chop very finely.

Ribbons: Vegetables shaved into ribbons using a peeler. If you have a spiralizer, this would work just as well.

Sauté: From the French verb *sauter*, meaning 'to jump'. Sautéed food is cooked in a small amount of fat, in an open pan on a high heat.

Thinly sliced: A sharp knife or a spiralizer is used to achieve thin slices.

Toasted nuts: Nuts heated in a medium-hot frying pan (without the addition of oil) to bring out the richness and flavour. Toast for a couple of minutes until fragrant, or light brown in colour.

Creamy Green Leafy

Get your greens with this tasty bowl of vegetable goodness

Ingredients

¼	**Onion** (sliced)
1 clove	**Garlic** (sliced)
1 tsp	**Olive Oil**
300ml	**Vegetable Stock** (½ cube)
40g	**Asparagus Tips** (quartered)
80g	**Broccoli** (florets)
⅙	**Courgette** (cubed)
1	handful **Spinach**
1 sprig	**Tarragon** (leaves, chopped)
1 tbsp	**Crème Fraîche** (half fat)

Preparation

1. Gently fry the **onions** and **garlic** in 1 tsp oil for 5 mins.

2. Pour in the **stock** along with **all the other veg** (except spinach). Bring to the boil, then simmer for 10 mins.

3. Mix through the **spinach** and **tarragon**, and cook for a couple of mins.

4. Blend until smooth. Serve topped with **crème fraîche**, black pepper and a few extra tarragon leaves.

130 Cals

2½ 5-a-day

6g Fibre

2g SatFat

8g Fat

7g Protein

9g Carbs

Size
Medium
435g

Recipe Tip
Can't get tarragon? Swap it for another fresh herb such as rosemary or oregano

Roasted Garlic & Asparagus

A smooth and simple asparagus soup with plenty of garlic

Ingredients

160g	**Asparagus**
¼	**Onion** (wedges)
6 cloves	**Garlic** (peeled)
1 tsp	**Olive Oil**
300ml	**Vegetable Stock** (½ cube)
few sprigs	**Chives**
6	**Basil** leaves
1 tbsp	**Crème Fraîche** (half fat)

Preparation

1. Coat the **asparagus**, **onion** and **garlic** in 1 tsp **oil** and roast at 160°C for 15 mins.

2. Blitz the roasted veg together with the **stock**, **herbs** and **crème fraîche**.

3. Serve sprinkled with black pepper and a few extra basil leaves.

10g Carbs	7g Protein	8g Fat	2g SatFat	6g Fibre	1½ 5-a-day	140 Cals

Nutrition Fact
Asparagus is an excellent source of folate, important during growth and pregnancy

Size
Small
400g

Broccoli & Fennel

The distinctive flavour of fennel gives this soup a pleasing lift

Ingredients

¼	**Onion** (sliced)
80g	**Fennel** (chopped)
1 tsp	**Olive Oil**
1 clove	**Garlic** (minced)
300ml	**Vegetable Stock** (½ cube)
120g	**Broccoli** (florets)
6	**Basil** leaves
1 sprig	**Parsley** (large)
1 tbsp	**Soured Cream**
¼	**Lemon** (juice only)

Preparation

1. Sauté the **onion** and **fennel** in 1 tsp **oil** for 10 mins. Add the **garlic** and cook for a further minute.

2. Pour in the **stock, broccoli,** and **herbs**. Cover and simmer for 8 mins or until the broccoli is tender.

3. Blitz in a blender until smooth.

4. Serve topped with extra basil leaves, **soured cream** and **lemon juice**.

145 Cals

2½ 5-a-day

9g Fibre

3g SatFat

8g Fat

8g Protein

10g Carbs

Size
Medium
435g

Recipe Tip
If you are dairy free, swap the soured cream for some chopped nuts

Creamy Garlic & Courgette

Velvety and light, this bowl of garlicky yumminess is sure to please

Ingredients

2/3	**Courgette** (chopped)
4 cloves	**Garlic** (in skin)
1 tsp	**Olive Oil**
1 tbsp	**Pine Nuts**
300ml	**Vegetable Stock** (½ cube)
1 sprig	**Parsley** (chopped)
1 tbsp	**Crème Fraîche** (half fat)

Preparation

1. Coat the **courgette** and **garlic** with 1 tsp **oil**, salt & pepper and roast at 180°C for 20 mins.

2. Gently dry fry the **pine nuts** until aromatic and starting to colour.

3. Heat the **stock** and add the roasted garlic (squeezed from its skin), courgette and **parsley** and simmer for a couple of minutes.

4. Remove from the heat, stir in the **crème fraîche**, then blend until smooth.

5. Serve topped with extra parsley and pine nuts.

6g Carbs	6g Protein	14g Fat	3g SatFat	3g Fibre	1 5-a-day	180 Cals

Nutrition Fact
At only 18 cals per 100g, courgette is a very low-calorie vegetable

Size
Small
395g

Fragrant Crab

This balanced blend of flavours has the unmistakable taste of Thailand

Ingredients

1 clove	**Garlic** (minced)	
1	**Spring Onion** (sliced)	
½ inch	**Ginger** (grated)	
1 tsp	**Chilli Oil**	
¼	**Red Pepper** (thinly sliced)	
400ml	**Vegetable Stock** (½ cube)	
50ml	**Coconut Milk** (tinned)	
2	**Kaffir Lime Leaves** (torn)	
¼	**Lime** (juice & zest)	
100g	**Crab** (tinned)	
1 sprig	**Coriander** (large, chopped)	
20g	**Cabbage** (shredded)	
40g	**Pak Choi** (chopped)	

Preparation

1. Fry the **garlic, spring onion** and **ginger** in 1 tsp **chilli oil** for 3 mins.
2. Add the **pepper** for 3 more mins.
3. Pour in the **stock** and **coconut milk**, and bring to the boil.
4. Stir in the **kaffir lime leaves, lime juice & zest**. Simmer for 5 mins.
5. Mix through the **crab, coriander, cabbage** and **pak choi**.
6. Simmer for 7 mins, then serve.

240 Cals

1½ 5-a-day

4g Fibre

8g SatFat

14g Fat

21g Protein

9g Carbs

Size
Medium
480g

Recipe Tip
Swap to low-fat coconut milk
to save 45 cals

Aubergine & Lemongrass

A curryesque combination of turmeric, lemongrass and coconut milk

Ingredients

⅛	**Onion** (diced)
1 tsp	**Sesame Oil**
1 clove	**Garlic** (minced)
½ inch	**Ginger** (grated)
¼	**Green Chilli** (thinly sliced)
1 tsp	**Lemongrass Paste**
pinch	**Turmeric** (ground)
120g	**Aubergine** (chopped)
300ml	**Vegetable Stock** (½ cube)
100ml	**Coconut Milk** (tinned)
1 tsp	**Fish Sauce**
1 sprig	**Coriander** (chopped)

Preparation

1. Fry the **onion** in 1 tsp **oil** for 5 mins, until soft.
2. Stir in the **garlic, ginger, chilli, lemongrass** and **turmeric**.
3. Add the **aubergine** for 3 mins.
4. Pour in the **stock, coconut milk** and **fish sauce**. Boil, then simmer for 10 mins.
5. Serve sprinkled with fresh **coriander** leaves.

10g Carbs	4g Protein	22g Fat	15g SatFat	4g Fibre	1½ 5-a-day	250 Cals

Recipe Tip
Swap the fish sauce for soy sauce to make this soup vegan

Size
Small
405g

Nutty Kale & Asparagus

The sprinkling of flaked almonds over this soup gives it a heavenly crunch

Ingredients

2 tbsp	**Flaked Almonds**
¼	**Onion** (diced)
2 tsp	**Olive Oil**
1 clove	**Garlic** (minced)
1 sprig	**Tarragon** (chopped)
1 sprig	**Thyme** (leaves, chopped)
80g	**Asparagus Tips**
2	handfuls **Kale**
400ml	**Vegetable Stock** (½ cube)
¼	**Lemon** (juice only)

Preparation

1. Dry fry the **flaked almonds** for 2 mins, then set aside.
2. Fry the **onion** in 2 tsp **oil**. Splash in a little water and allow to caramelise for 10 mins. Add **garlic** and **herbs** for 1 min.
3. Stir through the **asparagus**, **kale**, ¾ of the flaked almonds and **stock**.
4. Bring to the boil and simmer for 10 mins. Then blend to the desired consistency.
5. Serve sprinkled with a few tarragon leaves, remaining flaked almonds and **lemon juice**.

255 Cals	2 5-a-day	6g Fibre	2g SatFat	21g Fat	9g Protein	8g Carbs

Size
Medium
515g

Nutrition Fact
Kale is rich in lutein, an antioxidant that contributes to healthy eyes and skin

Creamy Brie & Mushroom

Ingredients

120g	**Mushrooms** (mixed, sliced)
2 tsp	**Olive Oil**
1 tsp	**Butter**
¼	**Onion** (diced)
½	**Celery** stalk (sliced)
1 clove	**Garlic** (sliced)
1 sprig	**Thyme** (leaves, chopped)
1 tsp	**Plain Flour**
300ml	**Vegetable Stock** (½ cube)
25g	**Brie** (cubed)
1 sprig	**Parsley** (large, chopped)
1 tbsp	**Crème Fraîche** (half fat)

Preparation

1. Fry the **mushrooms** in 2 tsp **oil** and 1 tsp **butter** for a few mins, until brown on both sides. Set aside.

2. In the same pan, gently sauté the **onion** and **celery** for 5 mins, then add the **garlic** and **thyme** for 1 min.

3. Stir through the **flour** for 2 mins, then pour in the **stock** (stirring gently). Boil, then simmer for 10 mins.

4. Add ¾ of the fried mushrooms to the soup, then blitz until smooth.

5. Add the **Brie** and stir until melted.

6. Serve topped with the remaining mushrooms, **parsley** and a swirl of **crème fraîche**.

8g	8g	23g	10g	3g		2	270
Carbs	Protein	Fat	SatFat	Fibre		5-a-day	Cals

Nutrition Fact
Mushrooms contain selenium, important for a healthy immune system

Size
Small
400g

Chilled Avocado Cucumber

Cool down with this delightful, chilled dish, which takes only moments to make

Ingredients

1	**Avocado** (flesh only)
½	**Cucumber** (peeled, seeds removed)
1 sprig	**Dill** (large)
1 clove	**Garlic**
50g	**Natural Yogurt** (full fat)
1	**Spring Onion** (halved)
150ml	**Water**
¼	**Lemon** (juice only)

Preparation

1. Blend **all the ingredients** (except the lemon juice) in a food processor until smooth.
2. Serve with a drizzle of **lemon juice** and a few extra dill leaves.

335 Cals

2½ 5-a-day

8g Fibre

7g SatFat

30g Fat

8g Protein

10g Carbs

Size
Medium
480g

Nutrition Fact
Avocados are packed with almost 20 different vitamins and minerals

Chicken, Lime & Avocado

Ingredients

1	**Spring Onion** (sliced)
¼	**Red Chilli** (thinly sliced)
1 clove	**Garlic** (finely sliced)
1 tsp	**Olive Oil**
300ml	**Chicken Stock** (½ cube)
40g	**Tomato** (cubed)
5	**Mint** leaves (torn)
100g	cooked **Chicken Breast** (shredded)
½	**Avocado** (cubed)
1 sprig	**Coriander** (chopped)
¼	**Lime** (juice only)

Preparation

1. Fry the **spring onions, chilli** and **garlic** in 1 tsp **oil** for 3 mins, stirring to avoid colouring.

2. Pour in the **stock, tomato** and **mint**. Bring to the boil.

3. Reduce to a simmer, then add the **chicken** and heat through for a few mins.

4. Remove from the heat and stir in the **avocado**.

5. Serve with chopped **coriander** and a squeeze of **lime juice**.

4g	35g	20g	4g	4g		1½	340
Carbs	Protein	Fat	SatFat	Fibre		5-a-day	Cals

Recipe Tip

Adding more or less chilli will have little effect on the nutritional content

Size
Medium
460g

Mushroom Ginger Broth

A light soup, packed with flavour...
and only 70 calories!

Ingredients

500ml	**Vegetable Stock** (½ cube)
120g	**Mixed Exotic Mushrooms** (sliced)
1 tbsp	**Light Soy Sauce**
2 inches	**Ginger** (grated)
½	**Spring Onion** (thinly sliced)
1 tsp	**Sesame Oil**

Preparation

1. Boil the **stock** with the **mushrooms, soy sauce** and **ginger**.

2. Lower the heat and simmer for 8 mins.

3. Serve topped with **spring onion** and drizzled with 1 tsp **sesame oil**.

70 Cals

1 5-a-day

1g Fibre

1g SatFat

5g Fat

2g Protein

4g Carbs

Size
Medium
455g

Nutrition Fact
Ginger is anti-inflammatory,
so great for joint pain and arthritis

Carrot & Orange

This vibrant soup will brighten up even the dullest mealtime

Ingredients

300ml **Water**
1½ **Carrots** (sliced)
⅛ **Onion** (chopped)
40g **Sweet Potato** (chopped)
½ **Orange** (zest only)
5 **Sage** leaves
30ml **Orange Juice** (fresh)

Preparation

1. Boil the **water** and add the **carrot, onion, sweet potato** and **orange zest**.

2. Lower the heat, add the **sage** leaves, cover and simmer for 15 mins, or until the vegetables are cooked.

3. Pour in the **orange juice**, remove the sage leaves, then blend to a smooth consistency.

4. Serve garnished with a few extra sage leaves.

22g	1g	1g	0g	6g	1½	95
Carbs	Protein	Fat	SatFat	Fibre	5-a-day	Cals

Recipe Tip

Make sure you zest the orange before cutting it for juicing

Size
Medium
440g

Gazpacho

A few drops of Tabasco provide the only heat in this classic chilled soup

Ingredients

160g	**Tomato** (chopped)
¼	**Cucumber** (cubed)
1 clove	**Garlic** (minced)
¼	**Onion** (diced)
½	**Red Pepper** (chopped)
few drops	**Tabasco**
¼	**Lemon** (juice only)
1 tsp	**Olive Oil**
3	**Basil** leaves

Preparation

1. Place the **tomato, cucumber, garlic, onion** and **pepper** in a blender and blitz until smooth.

2. Add the **Tabasco** and **lemon juice**, and season.

3. Serve drizzled with 1 tsp **olive oil**, a few extra cubes of cucumber and the **basil** leaves.

105 Cals

3½ 5-a-day

5g Fibre

1g SatFat

5g Fat

3g Protein

13g Carbs

Size
Medium
425g

Nutrition Fact
Tomatoes contain antioxidant lycopene, known to protect against heart disease

Kale & Greens

Apple contributes a touch of unexpected sweetness in this delicate dish

Ingredients

¼	**Onion** (diced)
1 tsp	**Olive Oil**
1 clove	**Garlic** (sliced)
¼	**Red Chilli** (sliced)
⅙	**Courgette** (cubed)
¼	**Red Apple** (peeled, cubed)
2	handfuls **Kale**
300ml	**Vegetable Stock** (½ cube)
1	handful **Spinach**
1 sprig	**Coriander** (chopped)
1 sprig	**Parsley** (large, chopped)

Preparation

1. Soften the **onions** in 1 tsp **oil** for 5 mins, over a low heat.
2. Mix in the **garlic, chilli, courgette** and **apple** and cook for 5 mins.
3. Add the **kale,** turn up the heat and sauté for 2 mins, until it starts to wilt.
4. Stir in the **stock, spinach** and half of the **herbs**. Simmer for 5 mins.
5. Blitz in a blender. Serve with remaining herbs and black pepper.

10g Carbs	4g Protein	6g Fat	1g SatFat	4g Fibre	2½ 5-a-day	110 Cals

Nutrition Fact
To absorb more iron from spinach, eat it with foods rich in vitamin C (e.g. peppers)

Size
Medium
465g

Tomato & Red Pepper

Half of your 5-a-day fruit & veg target for only 110 cals
- perfect for any low-calorie diet

Ingredients

¼	**Onion** (chopped)
¾	**Red Pepper** (diced)
1 tsp	**Olive Oil**
1 clove	**Garlic** (minced)
300ml	**Vegetable Stock** (½ cube)
120g	**Tomato** (diced)
6	**Basil** leaves (torn)
1 tsp	**Tomato Purée**

Preparation

1. Fry the **onion** and **pepper** in 1 tsp **oil** for 5 mins, then stir in the **garlic** for 1 min.

2. Pour in the **stock**, **tomato**, **basil** leaves and **tomato purée**. Simmer for 15 mins.

3. Blitz to a smooth consistency or leave chunky.

4. Serve with a few extra basil leaves.

110 Cals	2½ 5-a-day		5g Fibre	1g SatFat	5g Fat	3g Protein	14g Carbs

Size
Medium
440g

Nutrition Fact
Peppers contain vitamin B6, important for a healthy brain and nervous system

Carrot & Ginger

Sweet and spicy, this soup really hits the spot

Ingredients

¼	**Onion** (diced)
¼	**Celery** stalk (diced)
1 tsp	**Olive Oil**
2 inches	**Ginger** (sliced)
1 clove	**Garlic** (sliced)
1½	**Carrots** (chopped)
400ml	**Vegetable Stock** (½ cube)
pinch	**Nutmeg** (grated)

Preparation

1. Sauté the **onion** and **celery** in 1 tsp **oil** for 5 mins.

2. Stir in the **ginger**, **garlic** and **carrot**, and cook for a further 2 mins.

3. Pour in the **stock** and boil gently for 10 mins, until the vegetables are soft.

4. Blend to the desired consistency and serve with a grating of **nutmeg**.

15g	2g	6g	1g	6g		2	110
Carbs	Protein	Fat	SatFat	Fibre		5-a-day	Cals

Nutrition Fact

Nutmeg has been shown to have anti-bacterial properties

Size
Small
400g

Leek & Pea

Light and refreshing, with a hint of mint

Ingredients

80g	**Leeks** (thinly sliced)
1/8	**Onion** (finely diced)
1 tsp	**Olive Oil**
1 clove	**Garlic** (minced)
400ml	**Vegetable Stock** (½ cube)
80g	**Peas**
5	**Mint** leaves (torn)

Preparation

1. Sauté the **leek** and **onion** in 1 tsp **oil** for 5 mins, until beginning to soften.

2. Add the **garlic** for a further minute.

3. Pour in the **stock**, adding the **peas** and **mint** leaves. Simmer for 8 mins.

4. Serve topped with a few extra mint leaves.

115 Cals

2 5-a-day

6g Fibre

1g SatFat

6g Fat

6g Protein

10g Carbs

Size
Medium
435g

Recipe Tip
If using fresh peas (instead of frozen), halve the cooking time in step 3

Roasted Cauliflower Kale

Ingredients

120g	**Cauliflower** (florets)
1 tsp	**Olive Oil**
2	handfuls **Kale**
¼	**Onion** (diced)
1 clove	**Garlic** (minced)
½	**Celery** stalk (sliced)
300ml	**Vegetable Stock** (½ cube)
5	**Mint** leaves (torn)
1 sprig	**Parsley** (large, chopped)

Preparation

1. Mix the **cauliflower** with ½ tsp **oil** and roast at 180°C for 25 mins, or until the edges are browning.
2. Add half the **kale** and roast for 5 more minutes.
3. Sauté the **onion**, **garlic** and **celery** in ½ tsp oil for 5 mins.
4. Separate the roasted cauliflower and kale (set crispy kale aside). Add the cauliflower to the pan with the **stock**.
5. Bring to the boil, stir in the remaining (raw) kale and **herbs**. Simmer for 5 mins.
6. Blitz in a food processor until smooth. Serve with crispy kale.

10g	6g	6g	1g	6g		2½	115
Carbs	Protein	Fat	SatFat	Fibre		5-a-day	Cals

Nutrition Fact
One portion (80g) of cauliflower has 95% of the recommended intake of vitamin C

Size
Medium
440g

Tomato & Basil

What could be more comforting than a
steaming bowl of tomato soup?

Ingredients

160g	**Cherry Tomatoes**
1/6	**Red Onion** (wedges)
1 clove	**Garlic** (in skin)
1/2	**Carrot** (diced)
1 tsp	**Olive Oil**
1 tsp	**Balsamic Vinegar**
300ml	**Vegetable Stock** (1/2 cube)
1 tsp	**Tomato Purée**
12	**Basil** leaves

Preparation

1. Coat the **tomatoes, onion, garlic**
   and **carrot** with 1 tsp **oil**, 1 tsp
   balsamic vinegar, salt & pepper.

2. Roast at 160°C for 25 mins,
   turning half way. Once ready,
   squeeze the garlic out of its skin.

3. Boil the **stock** and add the tomato
   and carrot mix, **tomato purée** and
   basil leaves. Simmer for 5 mins.

4. Blend until smooth, adding
   extra water if needed.

5. Serve with a few extra basil leaves.

115 Cals

2 5-a-day

5g Fibre

1g SatFat

6g Fat

3g Protein

14g Carbs

Size
Medium
430g

Nutrition Fact
Tomatoes are rich in biotin, for healthy
skin, hair, eyes, liver and nervous system

Turmeric Tomato

Turmeric lends an unusual twist to classic tomato

Ingredients

1/3	**Red Onion** (diced)
1 clove	**Garlic** (minced)
1 tsp	**Olive Oil**
200ml	**Vegetable Stock** (½ cube)
80g	**Cherry Tomatoes** (halved)
200g	**Chopped Tomatoes** (tinned)
1 tsp	**White Wine Vinegar**
½ tsp	**Turmeric** (ground)
4	**Basil** leaves (torn)

Preparation

1. Fry the **onion** and **garlic** in 1 tsp **oil** for 5 mins, until starting to soften.
2. Pour in the **stock**, all the **tomatoes**, **vinegar** and **turmeric**.
3. Bring to the boil, then simmer for 10 mins, until cherry tomatoes are soft.
4. Blitz until smooth and serve topped with **basil** leaves.

15g Carbs	4g Protein	5g Fat	1g SatFat	4g Fibre	2½ 5-a-day	120 Cals

Nutrition Fact

Turmeric has been shown to improve indigestion, reducing bloating and gas

Size
Medium
450g

Tom Yum

A mouth-watering, Asian-inspired, spicy bowlful

Ingredients

½	**Carrot**	(thin strips)
40g	**Galangal**	(sliced)
1 clove	**Garlic**	(finely chopped)
1 inch	**Ginger**	(finely chopped)
½	**Lemongrass** stalk	(sliced)
¼	**Lime**	(juice only)
100g	**Prawns**	(raw)
½	**Red Chilli**	(finely sliced)
400ml	**Vegetable Stock**	(½ cube)
2	**Kaffir Lime Leaves**	(torn)

Preparation

1. Bring to the boil **all the ingredients** except the kaffir lime leaves.

2. Add the **kaffir lime leaves** and simmer for 3 mins, or until the prawns are cooked.

3. Serve and enjoy!

130 Cals	1 5-a-day		3g Fibre	0g SatFat	1g Fat	18g Protein	12g Carbs

Size
Small
395g

Nutrition Fact
Prawns are low in calories and high in good quality protein

Chilli Roasted Red Pepper

Roasting the pepper for this dish intensifies its scrumptiousness

Ingredients

1	**Red Pepper** (quartered)
2 tsp	**Olive Oil**
½	**Carrot** (sliced)
⅓	**Red Onion** (diced)
½	**Celery** stalk (sliced)
¼	**Red Chilli** (sliced)
1 clove	**Garlic** (minced)
300ml	**Vegetable Stock** (½ cube)
100g	**Chopped Tomatoes** (tinned)
1 sprig	**Parsley** (large, chopped)
pinch	**Chilli Flakes**

Preparation

1. Coat the **pepper** with 1 tsp **oil** and roast at 180°C for 15 mins, or until soft. Allow to cool.

2. Fry the **carrot**, **onion**, **celery**, **chilli** and **garlic** in 1 tsp oil for 5 mins.

3. Pour in the **stock**, **tomatoes** and pepper, bring to the boil and simmer for 10 mins.

4. Remove from the heat and blend.

5. Serve with **parsley** and a pinch of **chilli flakes**.

18g Carbs	4g Protein	9g Fat	1g SatFat	8g Fibre	3½ 5-a-day	165 Cals

Nutrition Fact
Peppers contain more vitamin C than oranges!

Size
Medium
440g

Earthy Mushroom

Ingredients

¼	**Onion** (finely diced)
½	**Celery** stalk (finely sliced)
½	**Carrot** (finely chopped)
1 tsp	**Olive Oil**
1 clove	**Garlic** (minced)
80g	**Chestnut Mushrooms**
10g	**Dried Mushrooms** (soaked, chopped)
300ml	**Vegetable Stock** (½ cube)
1 tsp	**Tomato Purée**
100g	**Chopped Tomatoes** (tinned)
1 sprig	**Rosemary** (leaves, chopped)
1 sprig	**Tarragon** (chopped)
40g	cooked **Puy Lentils**

Preparation

1. Fry the **onion**, **celery** and **carrot** in 1 tsp **oil** for 5 mins.

2. Stir in the **garlic** and **mushrooms** (strain the soaking liquid through muslin and save). Cook until any water from the mushrooms evaporates.

3. Pour in the **stock**, soaking liquid, **tomato purée**, **tomatoes** and **herbs**. Boil, then simmer for 5 mins.

4. Stir through the **puy lentils**, heat for 2 mins and serve.

185 Cals

4 5-a-day

9g Fibre

1g SatFat

7g Fat

10g Protein

21g Carbs

Size
Large
665g

Nutrition Fact
Mushrooms are as high in antioxidants as tomatoes, carrots and peppers

Butternut & Apple

Sweet & aromatic, this effortless soup is sure to satisfy

Ingredients

¼	**Onion** (diced)
1 tsp	**Olive Oil**
½	**Apple** (peeled, cubed)
160g	**Butternut Squash** (peeled, cubed)
½ tsp	**Cinnamon** (ground)
½ tsp	**Cumin** (ground)
½ tsp	**Ginger** (ground)
300ml	**Vegetable Stock** (½ cube)
1 tbsp	**Crème Fraîche** (half fat)

Preparation

1. Fry the **onion** in 1 tsp **oil** until starting to soften.
2. Add **all the remaining ingredients** (except the crème fraîche) and bring to the boil. Lower the heat and simmer for 20 mins.
3. Once the squash is tender, blend the soup until smooth.
4. Serve with black pepper and a swirl of **crème fraîche**.

28g Carbs	4g Protein	8g Fat	2g SatFat	6g Fibre	2½ 5-a-day	190 Cals

Nutrition Fact
Apples have a very high antioxidant content, compared to most fruit

Size
Medium
445g

Leek & Potato

Timeless, tasty and only 225 calories!

Ingredients

120g	**Leeks** (sliced)
1 clove	**Garlic** (minced)
1 tsp	**Butter**
1 tsp	**Olive Oil**
100g	**Potato** (diced)
1 sprig	**Thyme** (leaves, chopped)
300ml	**Chicken Stock** (½ cube)
1 tbsp	**Soured Cream**
few sprigs	**Chives** (chopped)

Preparation

1. Fry the **leeks** and **garlic** in 1 tsp **butter** and 1 tsp **oil** for 5 mins, stirring constantly to avoid burning or colouring.

2. Mix through the **potato** and **thyme** leaves and stir for a further minute.

3. Pour in the **stock**, bring to the boil, then simmer for 10 mins or until the potatoes are soft.

4. Blend to the desired consistency (or leave chunky).

5. Serve with a small dollop of **soured cream** and fresh **chives**.

225 Cals	1 5-a-day		6g Fibre	5g SatFat	12g Fat	5g Protein	25g Carbs

Size
Small
410g

Recipe Tip
Leave the skin on your potatoes for extra fibre (and save time peeling!)

Spicy Carrot & Lentil

Chilli & spices give this carrot soup a gentle kick

Ingredients

1 tsp	**Cumin Seeds**
1 tsp	**Olive Oil**
1½	**Carrots** (chopped)
1	**Celery** stalk (chopped)
¼	**Onion** (chopped)
1 clove	**Garlic** (minced)
½	**Red Chilli** (small, sliced)
30g	dried **Red Split Lentils**
400ml	**Vegetable Stock** (½ cube)
50g	**Greek Yogurt** (fat free)
1 sprig	**Coriander** (chopped)

Preparation

1. Dry fry the **cumin seeds** in a saucepan until aromatic.

2. Add 1 tsp **oil**, the **vegetables**, **garlic**, **chilli** and **lentils**, and fry for 3 mins.

3. Pour in the **stock**, bring to the boil and simmer for 15 mins, or until the lentils are swollen.

4. Blend until smooth if desired, or leave as a lovely broth.

5. Stir through the **Greek yogurt** and serve topped with **coriander**.

35g Carbs	13g Protein	6g Fat	1g SatFat	9g Fibre		3 5-a-day	240 Cals

Nutrition Fact

Lentils are high in both fibre and protein, so keep you feeling full for longer

Size
Medium
450g

Mushroom & Chestnut

The addition of chestnuts makes this mushroom soup especially moreish

Ingredients

¼	Onion (sliced)
1 tsp	Olive Oil
1 clove	Garlic (minced)
100g	Chestnut Mushrooms (diced)
50g	Chestnuts (chopped)
300ml	Vegetable Stock (½ cube)
1 tbsp	Crème Fraîche (half fat)
1 sprig	Thyme (leaves, chopped)
1 tbsp	Pine Nuts

Preparation

1. Gently fry the **onion** in 1 tsp **oil** for 5 mins, until starting to soften.

2. Increase the heat and add the **garlic** and **mushrooms**. Sauté for 5 mins, until the liquid from the mushrooms evaporates.

3. Stir in the **chestnuts** and **stock**. Simmer for 10 mins.

4. Blitz briefly, then stir in the **crème fraîche**.

5. Serve topped with **thyme** and **pine nuts**.

240 Cals

2 5-a-day

5g Fibre

3g SatFat

14g Fat

6g Protein

21g Carbs

Size
Small
400g

Nutrition Fact
Chestnuts are a source of manganese, which helps form connective tissue

Roasted Cauliflower

Roasting cauliflower unlocks its hidden flavour!

Ingredients

½ tsp	**Cumin Seeds**
2 cloves	**Garlic** (in skin)
160g	**Cauliflower** (florets)
2 tsp	**Olive Oil**
¼	**Onion** (sliced)
1 sprig	**Thyme** (leaves, chopped)
300ml	**Vegetable Stock** (½ cube)
1 tbsp	**Pine Nuts**
1 tbsp	**Crème Fraîche** (half fat)

Preparation

1. Toss the **cumin seeds**, **garlic** and **cauliflower** in 1 tsp **oil** and roast at 180°C for 30 mins, then set aside.

2. Fry the **onion** in 1 tsp oil for 5 mins. Then stir in the **thyme**.

3. Add ¾ of the roasted cauliflower, squeeze the garlic out of its skin and pour in the **stock**. Simmer for 5 mins.

4. Dry fry the **pine nuts** for a few mins, until fragrant, and set aside.

5. Blend soup with 1 tbsp **crème fraîche**, until smooth.

6. Serve topped with pine nuts and the remaining cauliflower.

13g	7g	19g	3g	5g
Carbs	Protein	Fat	SatFat	Fibre

1½ 5-a-day

245 Cals

Nutrition Fact

Pine nuts contain magnesium, important for normal muscle and nerve function

Size
Small
330g

Quick Noodle

Short on time? Whip up this beauty in under 15 minutes!

Ingredients

500ml	**Chicken Stock** (½ cube)
50g	dried **Wholewheat Noodles**
1	**Spring Onion** (finely sliced)
40g	**Mushrooms** (halved)
1 inch	**Ginger** (grated)
1 tsp	**Oyster Sauce**
1 tsp	**Light Soy Sauce**
40g	**Beansprouts**
40g	**Pak Choi** (sliced)
1 tsp	**Sesame Oil**

Preparation

1. Boil the **stock**, then add the **noodles**, **spring onion**, **mushrooms**, **ginger** and **sauces**.
2. Simmer for 5 mins, or until the noodles are tender, then stir in the **beansprouts** and **pak choi**.
3. Cover and cook for 2 mins.
4. Drizzle with **sesame oil** and serve.

250 Cals

1½ 5-a-day

5g Fibre

1g SatFat

6g Fat

10g Protein

41g Carbs

Size
Medium
525g

Nutrition Fact
Pak choi is a nutrient powerhouse, providing lots of nutrients for few calories

Red Cauliflower Cheese

Better wear a bib for this bright bowlful

Ingredients

½	**Red Pepper** (diced)
160g	**Cauliflower** (florets)
2 tsp	**Olive Oil**
⅓	**Red Onion** (sliced)
1 clove	**Garlic** (sliced)
300ml	**Chicken Stock** (½ cube)
80g	**Roasted Red Pepper** (from jar, sliced)
1 sprig	**Thyme** (leaves, chopped)
25g	**Goat's Cheese** (cubed)

Preparation

1. Toss the **fresh red pepper** and **cauliflower** in 1 tsp oil. Roast at 160°C for 20 mins, or until the vegetables are tender.

2. Sauté the **onion** in 1 tsp oil for 5 mins until softened, stirring to avoid browning. Add the **garlic** for a further minute.

3. Pour in the **stock**, roasted vegetables, **jarred red pepper** and **thyme**. Simmer for 10 mins, then stir in the **goat's cheese**.

4. Blend to the desired consistency and serve.

20g	12g	16g	6g	7g
Carbs	Protein	Fat	SatFat	Fibre

3½ 5-a-day

265 Cals

Nutrition Fact
Red peppers are high in beta-carotene, to avoid an itchy scalp and dry hair

Size
Medium
480g

Beetroot & Horseradish

This surprising mix of beetroot & horseradish
is full-flavoured and delicious

Ingredients

¼	**Onion** (diced)
1 tsp	**Olive Oil**
2	**Raw Beetroots** (cubed)
100g	**Potato** (cubed)
400ml	**Chicken Stock** (½ cube)
1 tbsp	**Horseradish Cream**
1 tbsp	**Soured Cream**

Preparation

1. Sauté the **onion** in
   1 tsp **oil** for 5 mins,
   until beginning to soften.

2. Add the **beetroot** and **potato**
   and fry for 2 mins before
   pouring in the **stock** and
   bringing to the boil.

3. Reduce the heat, cover and
   simmer for 25 mins, until
   the vegetables are cooked.

4. Blitz until smooth, then stir
   in the **horseradish cream**.

5. Serve with **soured cream**
   swirled through.

270 Cals

1½ 5-a-day

7g Fibre

3g SatFat

11g Fat

6g Protein

39g Carbs

Size
Small
420g

Nutrition Fact
Horseradish is rich in glucosinolates,
which may protect against cancer

Beetroot & Goat's Cheese

Creamy goat's cheese perfectly complements the sweet and earthy beetroot

Ingredients

2	**Raw Beetroots** (halved)
2 tsp	**Olive Oil**
½	**Carrot** (diced)
40g	**Leeks** (sliced)
40g	**Potato** (cubed)
1 clove	**Garlic** (minced)
1 sprig	**Thyme** (leaves, chopped)
300ml	**Vegetable Stock** (½ cube)
25g	**Goat's Cheese**

Preparation

1. Toss **beetroot** with 1 tsp **oil**, wrap in foil and cook at 160°C for 40 mins.
2. Fry the **carrot**, **leek** and **potato** in 1 tsp oil for 5 mins, then add the **garlic** and **thyme** for 1 min.
3. Pour in the **stock** with the roasted beetroot and simmer for 10 mins, or until the vegetables are soft.
4. Blitz in a food processor, then serve with crumbled **goat's cheese** and a few extra thyme leaves.

26g	10g	16g	6g	8g
Carbs	Protein	Fat	SatFat	Fibre

2	275
5-a-day	Cals

Nutrition Fact

Beetroot is rich in nitrates, which are beneficial for blood pressure

Size
Small
350g

Cauliflower & Caraway

Caraway seeds are a lively addition to this delicate cauliflower dish

Ingredients

½	**Onion** (diced)
2 tsp	**Caraway Seeds**
2 tsp	**Olive Oil**
100g	**Potato** (cubed)
160g	**Cauliflower** (florets)
300ml	**Vegetable Stock** (½ cube)
1 tbsp	**Crème Fraîche** (half fat)
1 sprig	**Parsley** (large, chopped)

Preparation

1. Gently fry the **onion** and **caraway seeds** in 2 tsp **oil** for 5 mins, until soft.

2. Add the **potato** and **cauliflower** and fry for a further 3 mins, before adding the **stock** and bringing to the boil.

3. Reduce the heat, cover and simmer for 10 mins, until the vegetables are tender.

4. Remove from the heat and blend until smooth.

5. Stir through the **crème fraîche** and **parsley**, and serve topped with a few caraway seeds.

280 Cals

2 5-a-day

7g Fibre

3g SatFat

12g Fat

8g Protein

36g Carbs

Size
Medium
475g

Recipe Tip
Love onion? Double the quantity in this recipe for only an extra 30 calories

Beetroot & Orange

Ingredients

½	**Carrot** (diced)	
⅓	**Red Onion** (diced)	
1 sprig	**Thyme** (leaves, chopped)	
1 tsp	**Olive Oil**	
300ml	**Vegetable Stock** (½ cube)	
1½	**Raw Beetroots** (cubed)	
½	**Orange** (zest only)	
75ml	**Orange Juice** (fresh)	
1 tbsp	**Pumpkin Seeds**	
80g	**Butter Beans** (tinned)	
1 tbsp	**Crème Fraîche** (half fat)	

Preparation

1. Sauté the **carrot**, **onion** and **thyme** in 1 tsp **oil** for 5 mins, until the onion starts to soften.

2. Pour in the **stock**, **beetroot**, **orange zest & juice**, and bring to the boil.

3. Cover and simmer for 20 mins, or until the beetroot is cooked.

4. Meanwhile, dry fry the **pumpkin seeds** for a few mins and set aside.

5. Add **butter beans** to the soup mix and warm through, then blend.

6. Serve topped with **crème fraîche** and pumpkin seeds.

35g Carbs	11g Protein	12g Fat	3g SatFat	11g Fibre	3½ 5-a-day	285 Cals

Recipe Tip
Omit the pumpkin seeds
to save 55 calories

Size
Medium
500g

Spiced Tahini Cauliflower

Ingredients

160g	**Cauliflower** (florets)
½ tsp	**Cumin Seeds**
2 cloves	**Garlic** (in skin)
¼	**Onion** (wedges)
3 tsp	**Olive Oil**
80g	**Potato** (cubed)
300ml	**Vegetable Stock** (½ cube)
pinch	**Turmeric** (ground)
1 tsp	**Tahini**
¼	**Lemon** (juice only)

Preparation

1. Coat the **cauliflower**, **cumin seeds**, **garlic** and **onion** in 2 tsp **oil** and roast at 180°C for 25 mins. Once cooked, squeeze the garlic out of its skin.

2. Sauté the **potato** in 1 tsp oil for 5 mins.

3. Add the cauliflower mix, **stock** and **turmeric**. Gently simmer for 10 mins, or until the vegetables are soft.

4. Remove from the heat and blend until smooth, adding extra water if needed.

5. Stir in the **tahini** and **lemon juice**, and serve.

285 Cals

1½ 5-a-day

6g Fibre

2g SatFat

17g Fat

8g Protein

28g Carbs

Size
Small
390g

Nutrition Fact
Tahini is made from sesame seeds, which contain more iron than beef liver

Potato, Cabbage & Bacon

Who says cabbage soup needs to be boring?
This one is sure to delight

Ingredients

¼	**Onion** (sliced)
½	**Celery** stalk (thinly sliced)
2	**Back Bacon** rashers (diced)
1 tsp	**Olive Oil**
100g	**Potato** (diced)
80g	**Green Cabbage** (shredded)
400ml	**Chicken Stock** (½ cube)
1 sprig	**Parsley** (chopped)

Preparation

1. Fry the **onion**, **celery** and **bacon** in 1 tsp **oil** for 5 mins, or until the onion starts to soften and the bacon browns.

2. Add the **potato** and cook for a further 2 mins before adding the **cabbage** and **stock**. Bring to the boil.

3. Lower the heat and simmer for 15 mins, or until the potato is cooked.

4. Serve with chopped **parsley**.

27g Carbs	15g Protein	15g Fat	4g SatFat	7g Fibre		2 5-a-day	295 Cals

Nutrition Fact
Cabbage is high in vitamin K, essential for building strong bones

Size
Medium
460g

Hot & Sour Pork & Tofu

Ingredients

500ml	Chicken Stock (½ cube)
1 inch	Ginger (thin strips)
1 clove	Garlic (thinly sliced)
1	Spring Onion (thinly sliced)
50g	Pork Shoulder (raw, lean, sliced)
80g	Button Mushrooms (sliced)
10g	Dried Mushrooms (soaked, sliced)
40g	Bamboo Shoots (tinned)
2 tsp	Sesame Oil
1 tsp	Light Soy Sauce
50g	Extra Firm Tofu (sliced)
1	Egg (whisked)
1 tsp	Balsamic Vinegar
1 sprig	Coriander (chopped)
pinch	White Pepper

Preparation

1. Boil the **stock** and add the **ginger, garlic** and ¾ of the **onion**. Simmer for 5 mins.

2. Add the **pork, mushrooms, bamboo shoots**, 1 tsp **oil** and **soy sauce** for 3 mins.

3. Add the **tofu** and cook for 1 more minute.

4. Stir in the middle of the pan to create a whirlpool and pour in the **egg** to form strands. Leave for a few seconds to allow the egg to cook in the hot soup.

5. Serve drizzled with 1 tsp sesame oil, **vinegar** and garnished with the **remaining ingredients**.

310 Cals	2 5-a-day		2g Fibre	4g SatFat	18g Fat	25g Protein	13g Carbs

Size
Medium
560g

Recipe Tip
To make this veggie, substitute the pork for extra tofu and use vegetable stock

Chicken Pho

Ingredients

35g	uncooked **Rice Noodles**
400ml	**Chicken Stock** (½ cube)
1 clove	**Garlic** (finely sliced)
½ inch	**Ginger** (grated)
1 clove	**Star Anise**
¼	**Red Chilli** (sliced)
1	**Spring Onion** (sliced)
100g	cooked **Chicken Breast** (shredded)
40g	**Beansprouts**
40g	**Pak Choi** (sliced)
1 tsp	**Fish Sauce**
¼	**Lime** (juice only)
1 sprig	**Coriander** (chopped)

Preparation

1. Cook the **noodles** as per the packet. Place in a serving bowl.

2. Boil the **stock** and add the **garlic, ginger, star anise, chilli** and half the **onion**. Simmer for 5 mins.

3. Stir in the **chicken, beansprouts** and **pak choi**. Heat for 2 mins.

4. Add the **fish sauce** and **lime juice**. Remove the star anise.

5. Pour the soup over the noodles. Serve topped with fresh **coriander** and the remaining spring onion.

34g Carbs	38g Protein	3g Fat	1g SatFat	2g Fibre

1½ 5-a-day   **315** Cals

Recipe Tip
A great way to use up leftover roast chicken

Size
Large
610g

Butternut Squash & Bacon

Maple syrup teamed with salty bacon makes this bowlful a taste sensation

Ingredients

120g	**Butternut Squash** (chopped)
1	**Carrot** (chopped)
2 tsp	**Olive Oil**
¼	**Onion** (diced)
1 clove	**Garlic** (minced)
1 tsp	**Maple Syrup**
300ml	**Chicken Stock** (½ cube)
pinch	**Nutmeg**
1 sprig	**Thyme** (leaves, chopped)
2	**Back Bacon** rashers (sliced)

Preparation

1. Coat the **squash** and **carrot** in 1 tsp **oil** and roast at 180°C for 30 mins, or until soft.
2. Fry the **onion** and **garlic** in 1 tsp oil for 5 mins.
3. Add the roasted veg, **maple syrup**, **stock**, **nutmeg** and **thyme**. Cook for 10 mins.
4. Meanwhile, dry fry the **bacon** until crispy.
5. Blitz the soup until smooth and serve topped with crispy bacon.

320 Cals

2½ 5-a-day

7g Fibre

5g SatFat

19g Fat

13g Protein

25g Carbs

Size
Small
395g

Recipe Tip
Roast the seeds from the centre of the butternut squash for a tasty snack

Pea & Ham

Ingredients

¼	**Onion** (diced)
1 clove	**Garlic** (sliced)
½	**Celery** stalk (sliced)
1 tsp	**Olive Oil**
500ml	**Chicken Stock** (½ cube)
40g	dried **Split Green Peas**
1	**Bay Leaf**
1 sprig	**Parsley** (large, chopped)
80g	**Petit Pois**
50g	cooked **Gammon** (shredded)
5	**Mint** leaves (torn)

Preparation

1. Fry the **onion**, **garlic** and **celery** in 1 tsp **oil** for 5 mins.

2. Pour in the **stock**, **split peas**, **bay leaf** and **parsley**. Bring to the boil and simmer for 25 mins, or until the peas soften.

3. Add the **petit pois**, heat for 1 min, then remove from the heat.

4. Blitz until smooth (you can add more liquid if you want a runnier consistency).

5. Serve with shredded **gammon**, **mint** and some extra parsley.

33g	26g	12g	3g	8g
Carbs	Protein	Fat	SatFat	Fibre

2½	340
5-a-day	Cals

Nutrition Fact
Peas contain a variety of nutrients beneficial for heart health

Size
Medium
490g

Leek, Parsnip & Bacon

With parsnip, bacon, mustard and apple,
every spoonful is packed with flavour

Ingredients

2	**Back Bacon** rashers
80g	**Leeks** (sliced)
1 tsp	**Olive Oil**
1 tsp	**Butter**
½	**Red Apple** (peeled, diced)
1½	**Parsnips** (diced)
300ml	**Chicken Stock** (½ cube)
1 tsp	**Wholegrain Mustard**

Preparation

1. Dry fry the **bacon** until crispy. Slice and set aside.
2. Meanwhile, fry the **leek** in 1 tsp **oil** and 1 tsp **butter** for 7 mins. Stir continuously to avoid browning.
3. Add the **apple** and **parsnip** for a further 3 mins.
4. Pour in the **stock** and simmer gently for 10 mins, or until the vegetables are soft.
5. Stir in the **mustard**, remove from the heat and blend to the desired consistency.
6. Serve the soup topped with crispy bacon.

350 Cals	**3** 5-a-day

9g Fibre	7g SatFat	21g Fat	15g Protein	27g Carbs

Size
Medium
505g

Nutrition Fact
Parsnips are rich in manganese, which is needed to produce sex hormones

Parsnip & Hazelnuts

Honey roasted veggies are the crowning glory of this bowl of scrumptiousness

Ingredients

½	**Carrot** (sliced)
¼	**Onion** (wedges)
1½	**Parsnips** (sliced)
40g	**Sweet Potato** (chopped)
2 tsp	**Olive Oil**
1 tbsp	**Honey**
1 tbsp	**Hazelnuts** (chopped)
400ml	**Vegetable Stock** (½ cube)
1 tbsp	**Crème Fraîche** (half fat)

Preparation

1. Coat the **vegetables** with 2 tsp **oil** and the **honey**. Roast at 180°C for 20 mins, or until soft.

2. Meanwhile, dry fry the **hazelnuts** for a couple of minutes.

3. Blend the roasted veg with the **stock** until smooth, before stirring in the **crème fraîche**.

4. Sprinkle with toasted hazelnuts and serve.

45g Carbs	6g Protein	19g Fat	3g SatFat	10g Fibre	2 5-a-day	360 Cals

Nutrition Fact
Hazelnuts are high in alpha tocopherol, which is protective against cancer

Size
Medium
500g

Spicy Beef Noodles

Ingredients

300ml	**Beef Stock** (½ cube)
1 clove	**Star Anise**
1	**Spring Onion** (sliced)
1 clove	**Garlic** (thinly sliced)
½ inch	**Ginger** (grated)
½	**Carrot** (chopped)
1	**Lemongrass** stalk
1 tsp	**Light Soy Sauce**
¼	**Red Chilli** (sliced)
100g	**Beef Rump** (raw, lean, sliced)
50g	dried **Wholewheat Noodles**
1 tsp	**Fish Sauce**
40g	**Sugar Snap Peas**
40g	**Pak Choi** (sliced)
1 sprig	**Coriander** (large, chopped)

Preparation

1. Boil the **stock** and drop in the **star anise**, **onion**, **garlic**, **ginger**, **carrot**, **lemongrass**, **soy sauce** and half the **chilli**.

2. Add the **beef** and **noodles**. Cover and simmer for 10 mins.

3. Stir in the **fish sauce**, **sugar snaps** and **pak choi**. Cook for a further 2 mins.

4. Remove the star anise and lemongrass. Serve with the remaining chilli and **coriander**.

360 Cals

2 5-a-day

6g Fibre

2g SatFat

6g Fat

32g Protein

46g Carbs

Size
Medium
590g

Nutrition Fact
Star anise has been shown to have anti-fungal and anti-viral properties

Goulash

Ingredients

¼ **Onion** (diced)
1 clove **Garlic** (minced)
½ **Carrot** (diced)
1 tsp **Olive Oil**
100g **Stewing Beef** (raw, lean, cubed)
400ml **Beef Stock** (½ cube)
pinch **Smoked Paprika**
½ **Red Pepper** (cubed)
25g uncooked **Pearl Barley**
100g **Chopped Tomatoes** (tinned)
1 tsp **Tomato Purée**
1 tbsp **Soured Cream**
1 sprig **Parsley** (chopped)

Preparation

1. Gently sauté the **onion**, **garlic** & **carrot** for 5 mins in 1 tsp **oil**.
2. Turn up the heat, stir in the **beef** and cook for 3 mins.
3. Pour in the **stock** along with the **paprika**, **pepper**, **pearl barley**, **tomatoes** and **tomato purée**.
4. Bring to the boil, then simmer for 20 mins.
5. Serve with a swirl of **soured cream** and a handful of **parsley**.

| 37g Carbs | 29g Protein | 12g Fat | 4g SatFat | 10g Fibre | 3 5-a-day | 360 Cals |

Nutrition Fact
Pearl Barley is low in fat and calories, but high in fibre

Size
Medium
435g

Chicken & Sweetcorn

Sometimes, nothing else but this simple dish will do -
it's a classic for a reason!

Ingredients

½ inch	**Ginger** (grated)
1 clove	**Garlic** (minced)
1	**Spring Onion** (sliced)
1 tsp	**Sesame Oil**
½ tsp	**Cornflour**
300ml	**Chicken Stock** (½ cube)
80g	**Sweetcorn** (tinned)
100g	cooked **Chicken Breast** (shredded)
1	**Egg** (whisked)
1 tsp	**Light Soy Sauce**

Preparation

1. Gently fry the **ginger**, **garlic** and half the **spring onion** in 1 tsp **oil** for 3 mins.

2. Make a **cornflour** paste with 1 tbsp **stock**. Add the paste to the pan along with the stock, stirring constantly until fully dissolved.

3. Add the **sweetcorn** and **chicken**. Cook for 2 mins then drizzle the **egg** into the soup while stirring, to form strands.

4. Serve with the remaining spring onions and a splash of **soy sauce**.

360 Cals

1 5-a-day

3g Fibre

3g SatFat

14g Fat

43g Protein

18g Carbs

Size
Small
420g

Nutrition Fact
Sweetcorn is rich in lutein and zeaxanthin, both beneficial for eye health

Sweet Potato & Coconut

This luscious ensemble of sweet potato, coconut and spices is a total taste explosion

Ingredients

¼	**Onion** (chopped)
1 clove	**Garlic** (minced)
1 inch	**Ginger** (grated)
½	**Celery** stalk (finely sliced)
1 tsp	**Olive Oil**
120g	**Sweet Potato** (cubed)
pinch	**Cayenne Pepper**
pinch	**Turmeric** (ground)
300ml	**Vegetable Stock** (½ cube)
100ml	**Coconut Milk** (tinned)
1 tbsp	**Flaked Almonds**
1 sprig	**Coriander** (chopped)

Preparation

1. Soften the **onion**, **garlic**, **ginger** and **celery** in a pan with 1 tsp **oil** for a few mins.

2. Mix in the **sweet potato**, **cayenne** and **turmeric**. Cook for 5 mins.

3. Pour in the **stock** and **coconut milk**, and bring to a gentle simmer for 12 mins, or until the potato is cooked.

4. Blend, then serve sprinkled with **flaked almonds** and **coriander**.

34g Carbs	6g Protein	28g Fat	16g SatFat	7g Fibre	1 5-a-day	400 Cals

Nutrition Fact

Sweet potato is a good source of vitamin D, for healthy bones, teeth and nerves

Size
Medium
485g

Chicken & Wild Rice

This hearty harvest is high in both protein & fibre, giving you a boost towards your daily targets

Ingredients

¼	**Onion** (diced)
½	**Celery** stalk (sliced)
½	**Carrot** (diced)
1 tsp	**Oregano** (dried)
1 tsp	**Olive Oil**
1 clove	**Garlic** (sliced)
600ml	**Chicken Stock** (½ cube)
35g	uncooked **Wild Rice**
100g	cooked **Chicken Breast** (shredded)
80g	**Peas**
1 sprig	**Parsley** (chopped)
1 sprig	**Thyme** (leaves, chopped)

Preparation

1. Gently fry the **onion, celery, carrot** and **oregano** in 1 tsp **oil** for 8 mins.
2. Stir in the **garlic** for 1 min, then pour in the **stock** and **rice**. Bring to the boil, and reduce to a simmer.
3. Cover and cook for 35 mins, or until the rice is tender (add more water if needed).
4. Mix through the **chicken, peas** and **herbs**, simmer for 2 mins and serve.

410 Cals

2½ 5-a-day

10g Fibre

2g SatFat

9g Fat

43g Protein

42g Carbs

Size
Medium
560g

Nutrition Fact
Wild rice contains more antioxidants than brown rice

Chunky Chicken & Chorizo

Pearl barley is used to thicken up this paprika pottage

Ingredients

25g	**Chorizo** (cubed)
¼	**Red Onion** (finely diced)
½	**Carrot** (finely diced)
80g	**Tomato** (chopped)
1 clove	**Garlic** (minced)
pinch	**Smoked Paprika**
1 tsp	**Olive Oil**
400ml	**Chicken Stock** (½ cube)
25g	uncooked **Pearl Barley**
1 sprig	**Parsley** (large, chopped)
100g	cooked **Chicken Breast** (shredded)

Preparation

1. Dry fry the **chorizo** until it starts to turn crispy. Set aside.
2. In the same pan, fry the **onion, carrot, tomato, garlic** and **paprika** in 1 tsp **oil** for 2 mins.
3. Add the **stock, barley,** chorizo and half the **parsley**. Cook until the barley is soft.
4. Add the **chicken** and warm through.
5. Serve sprinkled with the remaining parsley.

31g Carbs	42g Protein	16g Fat	4g SatFat	8g Fibre	2 5-a-day	425 Cals

Recipe Tip
To maximise nutrients and fibre, use wholegrain rather than pearl barley

Size
Medium
470g

Sweet Potato Blue Cheese

Sweet and salty, with a blue cheese tang...
when it comes to flavour, this one has it covered

Ingredients

80g	**Sweet Potato** (cubed)
1 tbsp	**Maple Syrup**
2 tsp	**Olive Oil**
¼	**Onion** (sliced)
1 clove	**Garlic** (sliced)
½	**Celery** stalk (sliced)
300ml	**Vegetable Stock** (½ cube)
1	**Pear** (quartered)
25g	**Dolcelatte** (crumbled)
1 tbsp	**Walnuts** (halved)

Preparation

1. Coat the **sweet potato** with the **maple syrup** and 1 tsp **oil**. Bake at 180°C for 15 mins.

2. Meanwhile, fry the **onion**, **garlic** and **celery** in 1 tsp oil for 5 mins, until translucent.

3. Add the **stock**, sweet potato and **pear**. Bring to a gentle boil, cover and simmer for 10 mins.

4. Remove from the heat and blitz until smooth.

5. Serve with crumbled **dolcelatte** and **walnuts**.

450 Cals	2 5-a-day		9g Fibre	8g SatFat	25g Fat	9g Protein	51g Carbs

Size
Medium
520g

Recipe Tip
If dolcelatte is not available, any blue cheese will work in this recipe

Palm Nut

Enjoy the flavours of palm fruit in this
traditional African stew

Ingredients

100g	**Beef Sirloin** (raw, lean, chunks)
400ml	**Chicken Stock** (½ cube)
¼	**Onion** (sliced)
1 clove	**Garlic** (sliced)
pinch	**Smoked Paprika**
½ tsp	**Black Pepper**
60g	**Palm Fruit Concentrate**
80g	**Tomato** (chopped)
10g	dried **Shrimp**
1	handful **Spinach**

Preparation

1. Boil the **beef** in the **stock** with
   the **onion, garlic, paprika**
   and **pepper** for 5 mins.

2. Add the **palm fruit, tomato** and
   shrimp. Simmer for 10 mins.

3. Stir through the **spinach**, heat
   for 5 more mins and serve.

13g Carbs	32g Protein	37g Fat	6g SatFat	4g Fibre

1½ 5-a-day

505 Cals

Nutrition Fact
Palm nuts are high in vitamin B3,
important for DNA repair

Size
Medium
580g

Winter Root Vegetable

Who says reaching your 5-a-day target is difficult?
This soup has all 5 portions for only 220 calories!

Ingredients

¼	**Onion** (diced)
1 clove	**Garlic** (sliced)
1 tsp	**Olive Oil**
80g	**Butternut Squash** (cubed)
1	**Carrot** (chopped)
80g	**Celeriac** (cubed)
2	handfuls **Kale**
1	**Parsnip** (chopped)
300ml	**Vegetable Stock** (½ cube)
1 sprig	**Thyme** (leaves)
1 tbsp	**Crème Fraîche** (half fat)

Preparation

1. Over a low heat, fry the **onion** and **garlic** in 1 tsp oil until they soften.

2. Add **all the veg** and sauté for a few mins before adding the **stock** and **thyme**. Bring to the boil.

3. Cover and simmer for 12 mins, until all the vegetables are cooked.

4. Blend to the desired consistency, adding more water if required.

5. Serve with **crème fraîche** stirred through.

220 Cals

5 5-a-day

15g Fibre

2g SatFat

9g Fat

7g Protein

30g Carbs

Size
Medium
475g

Nutrition Fact
Kale is a good source of manganese, which is essential for healthy bones

Tomato & Bean

This hearty, wholesome soup contains all 5 of your 5-a-day
and over half of your daily fibre needs!

Ingredients

40g	**Leeks** (thinly sliced)
½	**Celery** stalk (chopped)
1	**Carrot** (chopped)
1 clove	**Garlic** (minced)
1 sprig	**Rosemary** (leaves, chopped)
pinch	**Paprika**
1 tsp	**Olive Oil**
200g	**Chopped Tomatoes** (tinned)
500ml	**Vegetable Stock** (½ cube)
80g	**Butter Beans** (tinned)
80g	**Cannellini Beans** (tinned)
1	handful **Kale**

Preparation

1. Fry the **leek**, **celery**, **carrot**, **garlic**,
   rosemary and **paprika** in 1 tsp **oil**
   for 10 mins, until the veg softens.

2. Pour in the **tomatoes** and **stock**. Bring
   to the boil, then simmer for 10 mins.

3. Add the **beans** and bring back to the boil.

4. Finally, add the **kale**, cook
   for 1 min, then serve.

39g Carbs	15g Protein	7g Fat	1g SatFat	17g Fibre	5 5-a-day	270 Cals

Recipe Tip
Try different types of tinned beans to
increase the diversity of your diet

Size
Large
650g

Minestrone with Basil Pesto

A big bowl of pasta, pesto and loads of veggies!

Ingredients

80g	**Asparagus Tips** (halved)
6	**Basil** leaves (torn)
40g	**Fennel** (chopped)
1 clove	**Garlic** (finely sliced)
80g	**Green Beans** (halved)
80g	**Leeks** (sliced)
45g	uncooked **Macaroni**
5	**Mint** leaves (torn)
600ml	**Vegetable Stock** (½ cube)
40g	**Petit Pois**
⅓	**Courgette** (cubed)
1 tbsp	**Pesto**

Preparation

1. Combine **all the ingredients** (except the pesto, petit pois and courgette) in a pan and bring to the boil.

2. Cover and cook for 8 mins, or until the pasta and vegetables are almost cooked.

3. Add the **petit pois** and **courgette** and cook for a further few mins.

4. Stir through the **pesto** and serve.

325 Cals	5 5-a-day	13g Fibre	1g SatFat	10g Fat	16g Protein	47g Carbs

Size
Large
650g

Nutrition Fact
Green beans are rich in folate, needed for the production of red & white blood cells

Cheesy Roasted Veg

Roasting the vegetables brings out their flavours and the goat's cheese on top is a real treat!

Ingredients

80g	**Butternut Squash** (cubed)
1	**Carrot** (chopped)
1/3	**Courgette** (chopped)
1/2	**Parsnip** (chunks)
2/3	**Red Onion** (wedges)
1/4	**Red Pepper** (chopped)
2 cloves	**Garlic** (in skin)
1 tbsp	**Olive Oil**
6	**Sage** leaves (chopped)
300ml	**Vegetable Stock** (½ cube)
25g	**Goat's Cheese** (crumbled)

Preparation

1. Combine **all the vegetables** with the **garlic**, 1 tbsp **oil** and half the **sage**.

2. Roast at 180°C for 40 mins, or until tender.

3. Once cooked, transfer to a blender. Pour in the **stock** and whizz until smooth.

4. Serve sprinkled with the remaining sage and **goat's cheese**.

29g Carbs	11g Protein	20g Fat	6g SatFat	11g Fibre	5 5-a-day	335 Cals

Nutrition Fact
Red onions are high in quercetin, which is anti-inflammatory and heart healthy

Size
Medium
475g

Almond & Greens

You'll go nuts for this healthful bowl of green goodness

Ingredients

¼	**Onion** (diced)
1	**Celery** stalk (sliced)
1 tsp	**Olive Oil**
50g	**Potato** (cubed)
400ml	**Chicken Stock** (½ cube)
80g	**Broccoli** (florets)
80g	**Peas**
2	handfuls **Spinach**
4	large handfuls **Watercress**
1 tbsp	**Crème Fraîche**
1 tbsp	**Flaked Almonds**

Preparation

1. Fry the **onion** and **celery** in 1 tsp **oil** for 5 mins. Add the **potato** and cook for a few mins more.

2. Pour in the **stock** and add the **broccoli**. Bring to the boil and simmer for 10 mins.

3. Stir in the **peas**, **spinach** and **watercress**, and cook for 2 mins.

4. Meanwhile, dry fry the almonds until fragrant.

5. Blend the soup and serve topped with **crème fraîche** and crunchy **almonds**.

340 Cals

5 5-a-day

14g Fibre

6g SatFat

19g Fat

17g Protein

27g Carbs

Size
Medium
570g

Nutrition Fact
Watercress has been shown to be protective against osteoporosis

Sweet Gingered Vegetable

Pear and pistachio are a curious combo in this vegtastic delight

Ingredients

120g	**Butternut Squash** (cubed)
80g	**Celeriac** (cubed)
1	**Carrot** (cubed)
3 tsp	**Olive Oil**
½	**Onion** (chopped)
1 inch	**Ginger** (grated)
½	**Pear** (chopped)
300ml	**Vegetable Stock** (½ cube)
1 tbsp	**Crème Fraîche** (half fat)
pinch	**Nutmeg**
1 tbsp	**Pistachios** (shelled)

Preparation

1. Toss the **squash**, **celeriac** and **carrot** with 2 tsp **oil** and 2 tbsp water. Roast for 40 mins at 160°C.

2. Gently sauté the **onion** and **ginger** in 1 tsp oil, until starting to soften. Stir to avoid browning.

3. Mix in the **pear** and roasted veg. Cook for 5 mins, then add the **stock**.

4. Bring to the boil, then simmer for 5 mins, or until the pear is tender.

5. Blitz in a blender, then serve with a swirl of **crème fraîche**, a pinch of **nutmeg** and sprinkled with **pistachios**.

36g Carbs	6g Protein	22g Fat	4g SatFat	15g Fibre	5 5-a-day	355 Cals

Recipe Tip
Celeriac can be used as a delicious, low-calorie alternative to potato

Size
Medium
505g

Aubergine & Chickpea

Ingredients

¼	**Onion** (chopped)
¼	**Red Pepper** (chopped)
½ inch	**Ginger** (grated)
1 clove	**Garlic** (minced)
½ tsp	**Coriander** (ground)
½ tsp	**Cumin** (ground)
½ tsp	**Turmeric** (ground)
1 tsp	**Olive Oil**
120g	**Aubergine** (cubed)
80g	**Butternut Squash** (cubed)
80g	**Tomato** (chopped)
80g	**Chickpeas** (tinned)
300ml	**Vegetable Stock** (½ cube)
100ml	**Coconut Milk** (tinned)
¼	**Lime** (juice only)
1 sprig	**Coriander** (large, chopped)

Preparation

1. Gently fry the **onion**, **pepper**, **ginger**, **garlic** and **spices** for 5 minutes in 1 tsp **oil**.

2. Add the **aubergine**, **squash**, **tomato** and ¾ of the **chickpeas** for 3 mins.

3. Pour in the **stock** and **coconut milk**. Simmer for 15 mins.

4. Meanwhile, roast the remaining chickpeas for 15 mins at 180°C.

5. Blend and serve topped with **lime**, **coriander** and roasted chickpeas.

390 Cals

5 5-a-day

13g Fibre

16g SatFat

24g Fat

11g Protein

34g Carbs

Size
Large
655g

Nutrition Fact
Aubergine contains copper, essential for producing energy in your cells

Roasted Roots & Lentils

Ingredients

80g	**Butternut Squash** (cubed)
1	**Carrot** (chopped)
80g	**Cauliflower** (florets)
¼	**Onion**
1	**Parsnip** (chopped)
2 cloves	**Garlic** (in skin)
1 sprig	**Rosemary** (leaves)
1 sprig	**Thyme** (leaves)
2 tsp	**Olive Oil**
1	handful **Kale**
200ml	**Vegetable Stock** (½ cube)
120g	**Lentils** (tinned)
1 tsp	**Tomato Purée**
100g	**Chopped Tomatoes** (tinned)

Preparation

1. Roast **all the veg** (except kale and tomatoes) with the **garlic, rosemary, thyme** and 2 tsp **oil** at 180°C for 30 mins. Add the **kale** for the last 3 mins.
2. Once cooked, de-skin the garlic.
3. Heat the **stock** and mix in the **lentils, tomato purée, tomatoes** and roasted veg. Cook for a couple of mins.
4. Briefly blend until thick and lumpy.
5. Serve with extra thyme leaves.

57g	18g	11g	2g	18g
Carbs	Protein	Fat	SatFat	Fibre

7 5-a-day

390 Cals

Nutrition Fact
Lentils are rich in molybdenum, which may be protective against cancer

Size
Large
655g

Spicy Tomato & Lentil

Ingredients

1	**Carrot** (chopped)
1/3	**Red Onion** (chopped)
1 clove	**Garlic** (chopped)
1/2 tsp	**Cinnamon** (ground)
1/2 tsp	**Cumin Seeds**
1/2 tsp	**Turmeric** (ground)
1 tsp	**Olive Oil**
80g	**Tomato** (chopped)
1/2	**Red Pepper** (chopped)
300ml	**Vegetable Stock** (1/2 cube)
100ml	**Coconut Milk** (tinned)
100g	**Chopped Tomatoes** (tinned)
30g	dried **Red Split Lentils**
1	handful **Spinach**
1 sprig	**Coriander** (large, chopped)

Preparation

1. Fry the **carrots**, **onion**, **garlic** and **spices** in 1 tsp **oil** for 5 mins.
2. Stir in the **fresh tomato** and **pepper**. Cook for a few mins until they soften.
3. Pour in the **stock**, **coconut milk**, **tinned tomatoes** and **lentils**.
4. Bring back to the boil and simmer for 12 mins, or until the lentils are cooked.
5. Remove from the heat and blend.
6. Return to the pan and stir through the **spinach**, to wilt. Serve with **coriander**.

410 Cals

5 5-a-day

11g Fibre

15g SatFat

23g Fat

13g Protein

41g Carbs

Size
Large
630g

Recipe Tip
Love spinach? Double the quantity for only 5 extra calories!

Lentil, Cabbage & Chorizo

Paprika and chorizo bring a hint of
Spanish spiciness to this substantial soup

Ingredients

1	**Carrot** (diced)
1	**Celery** stalk (finely sliced)
½	**Onion** (finely chopped)
1 clove	**Garlic** (minced)
pinch	**Smoked Paprika**
50g	**Chorizo** (cubed)
1 tsp	**Olive Oil**
400ml	**Chicken Stock** (½ cube)
100g	**Chopped Tomatoes** (tinned)
½ tsp	**Oregano** (dried)
1 sprig	**Parsley** (large, chopped)
1 sprig	**Thyme** (chopped)
50g	dried **Red Split Lentils**
40g	**Cabbage** (shredded)

Preparation

1. Fry the **carrot, celery, onion, garlic, paprika** and **chorizo** in 1 tsp **oil** for 5 mins.

2. Pour in the **stock, tomatoes, herbs** and **lentils**. Bring to the boil, then simmer for 10 mins.

3. Stir in the **cabbage** and cook for 3 mins, adding extra water if needed.

50g Carbs	29g Protein	22g Fat	7g SatFat	14g Fibre

5 5-a-day	500 Cals

Nutrition Fact
High in soluble fibre, lentils can
help to reduce blood cholesterol

Size
Medium
550g

White Bean & Kale

Fulfilling your fibre requirement is easy - this soup has
nearly half your daily target for just 225 cals!

Ingredients

¼	**Onion** (finely diced)
1 clove	**Garlic** (minced)
½	**Carrot** (finely chopped)
½	**Celery** stalk (diced)
½ tsp	**Oregano** (dried)
1 tsp	**Olive Oil**
300ml	**Vegetable Stock** (½ cube)
2	handfuls **Kale**
100g	**Chopped Tomatoes** (tinned)
1 sprig	**Rosemary** (leaves, chopped)
120g	**Cannellini Beans** (tinned)
1 sprig	**Thyme** (leaves, chopped)

Preparation

1. Fry the **onion, garlic, carrot, celery** and **oregano** in 1 tsp **oil** for 5 mins until soft.

2. Add the **stock, kale, tomatoes** and **rosemary** and cook for 5 mins, or until the vegetables are tender.

3. Mix through the **beans** and **thyme**. Heat for 2 mins before serving.

225 Cals

4 5-a-day

14g Fibre

1g SatFat

6g Fat

13g Protein

30g Carbs

Size
Medium
545g

Recipe Tip
If you have no cannellini beans, substitute for any other variety of beans

Green Lemon Lentil

Love it lemony? This summery jumble will tickle your tongue in all the right places

Ingredients

40g	**Leeks** (thinly sliced)	
1 clove	**Garlic** (minced)	
1 tsp	**Olive Oil**	
80g	**Broccoli** (small florets)	
40g	**Cabbage** (thinly sliced)	
1/6	**Courgette** (cubed)	
1/4	**Lemon** (peel only)	
400ml	**Vegetable Stock** (½ cube)	
5	**Mint** leaves (torn)	
120g	**Lentils** (tinned)	
½	**Lemon** (juice only)	

Preparation

1. Fry the **leek** and **garlic** in 1 tsp **oil** for 5 mins until soft.
2. Add the chopped **veg** and **lemon peel**, and stir-fry for 2 mins.
3. Pour in the **stock** and add **mint** leaves. Cover and cook for 10 mins.
4. Mix in the **lentils**, heat for 2 mins, then squeeze over the **lemon juice**.
5. Serve with a slice of lemon and a few extra mint leaves.

29g	16g	6g	1g	11g		3½	225
Carbs	Protein	Fat	SatFat	Fibre		5-a-day	Cals

Nutrition Fact
Mint has one of the highest antioxidant capacities of any food

Size
Large
685g

Black Eye Avocado

This nutritious dish has nearly half your daily fibre and 4 of your 5-a-day... not bad for under 250 cals!

Ingredients

½ tsp	**Cumin Seeds**
1 tsp	**Olive Oil**
¼	**Onion** (finely chopped)
½	**Green Chilli** (sliced)
1 clove	**Garlic** (minced)
pinch	**Cayenne Pepper**
½ tsp	**Chilli Powder**
300ml	**Vegetable Stock** (½ cube)
80g	**Black Eye Beans** (tinned)
½	**Carrot** (finely chopped)
⅙	**Courgette** (diced)
¼	**Green Pepper** (chopped)
40g	**Sweetcorn** (tinned)
1 sprig	**Coriander** (chopped)
¼	**Avocado** (cubed)

Preparation

1. Fry the **cumin seeds** in 1 tsp **oil** until aromatic.
2. Add the **onion**, **chilli**, **garlic** and remaining **spices** for 5 mins.
3. Pour in the **stock**, **beans** and **vegetables** (except the avocado).
4. Boil, then simmer for 15 mins, or until the vegetables are tender.
5. Top with **coriander** and **avocado**.

245 Cals

4 5-a-day

13g Fibre

2g SatFat

13g Fat

8g Protein

22g Carbs

Size
Medium
460g

Nutrition Fact
Black beans have been shown to help prevent heart disease

Spicy Sweetcorn Pancetta

Set alight your appetite with this vibrant dish

Ingredients

¼	**Onion**	(diced)
1	**Red Chilli**	(sliced)
1 clove	**Garlic**	(sliced)
1	**Celery**	stalk (sliced)
½ tsp	**Coriander**	(ground)
1 tsp	**Olive Oil**	
300ml	**Chicken Stock**	(½ cube)
160g	**Butternut Squash**	(cubed)
160g	**Sweetcorn**	(tinned)
2	**Pancetta**	slices (torn)

Preparation

1. Fry the **onion, chilli, garlic, celery** and **coriander** in 1 tsp **oil** for 5 mins.
2. Pour in the **stock** with the **squash**. Cover and cook for 15 mins.
3. Mix through the **sweetcorn**, lower the heat and simmer for 3 mins, or until the squash is soft.
4. Meanwhile, dry fry the **pancetta** until crispy.
5. Blend to the desired consistency, then serve topped with pancetta.

41g Carbs	9g Protein	10g Fat	2g SatFat	11g Fibre		3½ 5-a-day	275 Cals

Nutrition Fact
200g butternut squash contains 437% of your daily vitamin A requirements!

Size
Medium
555g

Sweet Celeriac

You can't go wrong with a bowl of parsnip yumminess - it's sure to put a smile on your face!

Ingredients

¼	**Onion** (sliced)
1 tsp	**Olive Oil**
1 tsp	**Butter**
120g	**Celeriac** (diced)
1	**Parsnip** (cubed)
400ml	**Vegetable Stock** (½ cube)
1 sprig	**Thyme** (leaves)
½	**Red Apple** (peeled, sliced)
1 tbsp	**Walnuts** (chopped)

Preparation

1. Gently sauté the **onion** in 1 tsp **oil** and 1 tsp **butter** for 5 mins.

2. Add the **celeriac** and **parsnip** and cook for a further 2 mins, stirring regularly.

3. Pour in the **stock**, **thyme** and **apple**. Cover, and cook for 10 mins until the vegetables are tender.

4. Blitz in a blender and serve sprinkled with **walnuts**.

280 Cals	3½ 5-a-day	12g Fibre	4g SatFat	17g Fat	6g Protein	26g Carbs

Size
Medium
490g

Nutrition Fact
Walnuts are anti-inflammatory, so great for those with joint pain and arthritis

Quinoa Chickpea Spinach

Packed with vitamins and full of flavour, this salubrious soup will really hit the spot!

Ingredients

⅓	**Red Onion**	(diced)
1 clove	**Garlic**	(minced)
1 tsp	**Oregano**	(dried)
1	**Carrot**	(diced)
40g	**Butternut Squash**	(cubed)
1 tsp	**Olive Oil**	
100g	**Chopped Tomatoes**	(tinned)
400ml	**Vegetable Stock**	(½ cube)
20g	uncooked **Quinoa**	(rinsed)
1 sprig	**Rosemary**	(leaves, chopped)
1 sprig	**Thyme**	(leaves, chopped)
80g	**Chickpeas**	(tinned)
2	handfuls **Spinach**	

Preparation

1. Fry the **onion, garlic, oregano, carrot** and **squash** in 1 tsp **oil** for 5 mins, or until the onion is soft.

2. Pour in the **tomatoes, stock, quinoa** and **herbs**, and bring to boil.

3. Simmer for 15 mins, or until the vegetables and quinoa are cooked.

4. Remove from the heat. Stir in the **chickpeas** and **spinach**, and cover with a lid for 3 mins, to allow the spinach to wilt.

42g	13g	9g	1g	13g	4½	285
Carbs	Protein	Fat	SatFat	Fibre	5-a-day	Cals

Nutrition Fact

Quinoa contains all 9 essential amino acids, used by the body to build protein

Size
Medium
515g

Bean & Barley

This bean bonanza delivers 15g fibre for just over 300 cals - perfect for a filling lunch

Ingredients

¼	**Onion** (diced)
1 clove	**Garlic** (sliced)
½	**Carrot** (chopped)
40g	**Fennel** (chopped)
pinch	**Basil** (dried)
1 tsp	**Olive Oil**
100g	**Chopped Tomatoes** (tinned)
400ml	**Vegetable Stock** (½ cube)
1	**Bay Leaf**
1 sprig	**Thyme** (leaves, chopped)
25g	uncooked **Pearl Barley**
40g	**Peas**
40g	**Black Eye Beans** (tinned)
40g	**Cannellini Beans** (tinned)

Preparation

1. Sauté the **onion, garlic, carrot, fennel & basil** in 1 tsp **oil** for 5 mins.
2. Pour in the **tomatoes, stock, herbs** and **pearl barley**. Cook for 30 mins, or until the barley is cooked.
3. Remove the bay leaf. Blend half the mixture, then return to the pan.
4. Stir in the **peas** and **beans**, heat through for a few mins and serve.

305 Cals

4 5-a-day

15g Fibre

1g SatFat

6g Fat

13g Protein

50g Carbs

Size
Medium
470g

Nutrition Fact
Thyme has been shown to have anti-bacterial and anti-fungal properties

Rustic Lentil & Potato

If you're feeling a bit chilly, wrap your hands around this lovely bowl of lentil stew

Ingredients

⅛	Onion (diced)
1 tsp	Olive Oil
1 clove	Garlic (minced)
½	Carrot (chopped)
100g	Potato (diced)
40g	Mushrooms (halved)
pinch	Thyme (dried)
400ml	Vegetable Stock (½ cube)
1 tbsp	Light Soy Sauce
60g	dried Green Lentils (rinsed)
20g	Cabbage (shredded)
1 sprig	Parsley (large, chopped)

Preparation

1. Sauté the **onion** in 1 tsp **oil** for 5 mins.
2. Stir in the **garlic, carrot, potato, mushroom** and **thyme** for 2 mins.
3. Pour in the **stock, soy sauce** and **lentils**. Simmer, covered, for 20 mins.
4. Add the **cabbage**, cover and simmer for 10 mins, or until the lentils are soft (add more water if needed).
5. Stir through the **parsley** and serve.

59g	19g	6g	1g	13g
Carbs	Protein	Fat	SatFat	Fibre

3 5-a-day

350 Cals

Nutrition Fact
Parsley is believed to be protective against cancer

Size
Medium
590g

Sausage Bean Broth

Simmering herbs create a flavoursome broth,
worthy of a tasty sausage

Ingredients

1	**Pork Sausage**
¼	**Onion** (diced)
1 clove	**Garlic** (finely sliced)
1 sprig	**Rosemary** (leaves, chopped)
½	**Celery** stalk (finely sliced)
80g	**Cabbage** (shredded)
½	**Carrot** (diced)
1 tsp	**Olive Oil**
300ml	**Chicken Stock** (½ cube)
1 sprig	**Thyme** (leaves, chopped)
1	**Bay Leaf**
80g	**Butter Beans** (tinned)

Preparation

1. Dry fry or grill the **sausage** for 7 mins, until the edges brown. Slice and set aside.
2. Sauté the **onion, garlic, rosemary, celery, cabbage** and **carrot** in 1 tsp **oil** for 5 mins.
3. Pour in the **stock** with the **thyme, bay leaf** and sausage. Simmer gently for 20 mins.
4. Stir in the **beans**, heat through and serve.

375 Cals

3½ 5-a-day

14g Fibre

7g SatFat

23g Fat

16g Protein

28g Carbs

Size
Medium
465g

Recipe Tip
To make this recipe vegetarian, use a veggie sausage and vegetable stock

Chorizo, Rice & Bean

Super hearty, this tempting chorizo dish will leave you licking your lips

Ingredients

50g	**Chorizo** (sliced)	
¼	**Onion** (finely chopped)	
1 clove	**Garlic** (minced)	
½	**Celery** stalk (chopped)	
100g	**Chopped Tomatoes** (tinned)	
500ml	**Beef Stock** (½ cube)	
35g	uncooked **Wild Rice**	
40g	**Roasted Red Peppers** (from jar, sliced)	
80g	**Kidney Beans** (tinned)	
1 sprig	**Parsley** (large, chopped)	
1 sprig	**Thyme** (large, chopped)	
¼	**Lime** (juice only)	

Preparation

1. Heat **chorizo** in a pan until the oils are released, then set aside.
2. Fry the **onion**, **garlic** and **celery** in the chorizo oil for 5 mins.
3. Pour in the **tomatoes**, **stock**, **rice**, **peppers**, **beans** and chorizo. Simmer for 20 mins, or until the rice is cooked (adding more water if needed).
4. Serve sprinkled with the **herbs** and a squeeze of **lime**.

51g Carbs	25g Protein	18g Fat	6g SatFat	12g Fibre

3½ 5-a-day

450 Cals

Recipe Tip
Add more lime juice if you like a tangier punch of citrus

Size
Medium
480g

Spring Chicken

This tasty chicken soup packs a whopping 44g protein for under 300 calories!

Ingredients

1 clove	Garlic (minced)
1/6	Red Onion (sliced)
1/2	Carrot (sliced)
1/2	Celery stalk (sliced)
1 tsp	Olive Oil
400ml	Chicken Stock (1/2 cube)
150g	Chicken Breast (raw, skinless, sliced)
80g	Broccoli (small florets)
20g	Cabbage (sliced)
40g	Peas
1 sprig	Parsley (large, chopped)
1 sprig	Thyme (leaves, chopped)

Preparation

1. Fry the **garlic**, **onion**, **carrot** and **celery** in 1 tsp **oil**, until softened.
2. Pour in the **stock** and **chicken**. Simmer for 8 mins, or until the chicken is cooked through.
3. Stir in the **broccoli** and cook for 2 mins before folding in the **cabbage**, **peas** and **herbs**.
4. Heat for a final 2 minutes before serving.

295 Cals

3 5-a-day

9g Fibre

1g SatFat

8g Fat

44g Protein

14g Carbs

Size
Medium
550g

Nutrition Fact
Lean meat and a variety of vegetables make chicken soup a perfect pick-me-up

Broccoli & Stilton

When you stick with the classics, you just can't go wrong - easy to make and tastes great!

Ingredients

¼	**Onion** (sliced)
1 clove	**Garlic** (sliced)
1 sprig	**Thyme** (leaves, chopped)
½	**Celery** stalk (sliced)
40g	**Potato** (cubed)
1 tsp	**Olive Oil**
400ml	**Vegetable Stock** (½ cube)
160g	**Broccoli** (small florets)
50g	**Stilton** (crumbled)

Preparation

1. Sauté the **onion**, **garlic**, **thyme**, **celery** and **potato** in 1 tsp **oil** for 5 mins.

2. Pour in the **stock** with the **broccoli** and simmer for 15 mins, or until all the vegetables are cooked.

3. Remove from the heat and blitz to the desired consistency. Add half the **Stilton** and allow to melt.

4. Serve topped with the remaining cheese and a few extra thyme sprigs.

18g	21g	23g	12g	9g		2	355
Carbs	Protein	Fat	SatFat	Fibre		5-a-day	Cals

Nutrition Fact
Minerals found in broccoli have been shown to impede the growth of cancer cells

Size
Small
415g

Peanut Butter Thyme

Ingredients

2 tsp	**Groundnut or Olive Oil**
½ tsp	**Chilli Powder**
pinch	**Thyme** (dried)
1 inch	**Ginger** (grated)
1 clove	**Garlic** (minced)
150g	**Chicken Breast** (raw, skinless, diced)
¼	**Onion** (diced)
¼	**Red Pepper** (chopped)
300ml	**Chicken Stock** (½ cube)
4 tsp	**Peanut Butter**
40g	**Tomato** (chopped)
1	handful **Baby Spinach**

Preparation

1. Use the **oil**, **chilli powder**, **thyme**, **ginger**, **garlic**, salt and pepper to thoroughly coat the **chicken**.

2. Allow to marinade for at least 15 mins.

3. Fry the chicken mixture until the chicken starts to brown.

4. Add the **onion** and **peppers** for a further 5 mins. Then pour in the **stock**, **peanut butter** and **tomato**.

5. Bring to the boil, cover and simmer for 15 mins. Remove the lid and simmer uncovered for 5 mins more.

6. Stir in the **spinach** and serve.

400 Cals

2 5-a-day

4g Fibre

3g SatFat

20g Fat

43g Protein

11g Carbs

Size
Small
380g

Nutrition Fact
It has been shown that those who eat nuts often are less likely to die of any disease

Pesto Chicken Pasta

We've made a dinnertime favourite into a scrumptious soup!

Ingredients

500ml	**Chicken Stock** (½ cube)
45g	uncooked **Wholemeal Pasta**
⅙	**Courgette** (cubed)
40g	**Green Beans** (halved)
40g	**Peas**
1 tbsp	**Pesto**
100g	cooked **Chicken Breast** (shredded)
6	**Basil** leaves (torn)
¼	**Lemon** (juice only)

Preparation

1. Boil the **stock** and add the **pasta**. Cover and simmer for 5 mins.
2. Add the **veg** with the **pesto** and cook for a further 7 minutes.
3. Stir in the **chicken** for 2 mins, warming through.
4. Serve with **basil** leaves and drizzled with **lemon juice**.

37g	43g	11g	2g	9g		1½	405
Carbs	Protein	Fat	SatFat	Fibre		5-a-day	Cals

Nutrition Fact
Wholewheat pasta contains twice as much fibre and B vitamins as white pasta

Size
Large
605g

Lamb & Pearl Barley

Succulent lamb and rosemary with an assortment of veggies. Get stuck in!

Ingredients

100g	**Stewing Lamb** (raw, lean, cubed)
1 tsp	**Olive Oil**
¼	**Onion** (finely diced)
1 clove	**Garlic** (minced)
1 sprig	**Rosemary** (leaves, chopped)
½	**Celery** stalk (finely diced)
½	**Carrot** (finely chopped)
40g	**Mushrooms** (quartered)
500ml	**Beef Stock** (½ cube)
1 tsp	**Tomato Purée**
25g	uncooked **Pearl Barley**

Preparation

1. Fry the **lamb** in 1 tsp **oil** for 5 mins, until starting to brown on all sides.
2. Add the **onion**, **garlic**, **rosemary**, **celery**, **carrot** and **mushrooms** for 5 mins.
3. Pour in the **stock**, **tomato purée** and **pearl barley**. Bring to the boil.
4. Lower the heat and simmer for 25 mins, or until the lamb and pearl barley are tender.

415 Cals

2 5-a-day

8g Fibre

7g SatFat

20g Fat

31g Protein

30g Carbs

Size
Medium
460g

Nutrition Fact
Rosemary has been shown to improve memory and concentration

Moroccan Harira Chickpea

Ingredients

¼	**Onion** (finely diced)
1 clove	**Garlic** (minced)
½ tsp	**Cinnamon** (ground)
½ tsp	**Cumin** (ground)
pinch	**Ginger** (ground)
pinch	**Nutmeg** (grated)
pinch	**Saffron**
½ tsp	**Smoked Paprika**
½	**Carrot** (finely chopped)
½	**Celery** stalk (finely diced)
2 tsp	**Olive Oil**
1 tsp	**Tomato Purée**
400ml	**Vegetable Stock** (½ cube)
1 tsp	**Honey**
120g	**Chickpeas** (tinned)
40g	dried **Green Lentils** (rinsed)
40g	**Tomato** (chopped)
1 sprig	**Parsley** (large, chopped)
1 sprig	**Coriander** (large, chopped)

Preparation

1. Fry the **onion**, **garlic**, **spices**, **carrot** and **celery** in 2 tsp **oil** for 5 mins, until soft.

2. Stir through **tomato purée**, pour in the **stock**, **honey**, **chickpeas**, **lentils** and **tomato**. Bring to the boil.

3. Cover and simmer for 15 mins, or until the lentils are cooked. Add more water if needed.

4. Stir in the **parsley** and **coriander**. Serve topped with a few extra herbs.

55g Carbs	21g Protein	14g Fat	2g SatFat	17g Fibre	3½ 5-a-day	415 Cals

Nutrition Fact

For a vegan soup, substitute the honey for agave, coconut or date syrup

Size
Medium
550g

Spicy Mussel & Saffron

Ingredients

¼	**Onion** (thinly sliced)
1 clove	**Garlic** (minced)
½	**Celery** stalk (finely sliced)
2 tsp	**Butter**
1 tsp	**Olive Oil**
100ml	**White Wine**
1 sprig	**Parsley** (large, chopped)
40g	**Tomato** (diced)
400ml	**Fish Stock** (½ cube)
pinch	**Saffron**
200g	**Mussels** (cleaned)
pinch	**Cayenne Pepper**
few sprigs	**Chives** (chopped)
1 tbsp	**Crème Fraîche**
¼	**Lemon** (juice only)

Preparation

1. Gently sauté the **onion**, **garlic** and **celery** in 2 tsp **butter** and 1 tsp **oil** until softened.

2. Drizzle with **wine**. Heat until the wine reduces.

3. Stir in the **parsley**, **tomato** and **stock**. Bring to the boil and add the **saffron**.

4. Mix through the **mussels**, cover and cook for 5 mins, or until all of the shells open.

5. Serve with the **cayenne**, **chives**, **crème fraîche** and **lemon juice**.

425 Cals

1½ 5-a-day

3g Fibre

11g SatFat

23g Fat

26g Protein

14g Carbs

Size
Medium
560g

Nutrition Fact

Mussels are higher in omega-3 (important for brain function) than other shellfish

Mediterranean Lentil

High in both protein and fibre, this delicious vegetarian soup will keep you full for hours!

Ingredients

1 clove	**Garlic** (minced)	
¼	**Onion** (finely chopped)	
1	**Carrot** (finely chopped)	
½	**Celery** stalk (finely chopped)	
1 tsp	**Oregano** (dried)	
1 tsp	**Olive Oil**	
100g	**Chopped Tomatoes** (tinned)	
40g	**Butternut Squash** (cubed)	
80g	dried **Red Split Lentils**	
400ml	**Vegetable Stock** (½ cube)	
1 sprig	**Parsley** (large, chopped)	
2	handfuls **Spinach**	
50g	**Greek Yogurt**	

Preparation

1. Fry the **garlic, onion, carrot, celery** and **oregano** in 1 tsp **oil** for 5 minutes.
2. Add the **tomatoes, squash, lentils** and **stock**. Cook for 15 mins, or until the veg and lentils are cooked.
3. Stir in the **parsley** and **spinach** to wilt.
4. Blend half the mixture and return to the pan. Stir through the **yogurt** and serve.

65g	28g	10g	4g	15g		5	445
Carbs	Protein	Fat	SatFat	Fibre		5-a-day	Cals

Nutrition Fact
Spinach contains antioxidants, which contribute to a healthy immune system

Size
Medium
530g

Creamy Chicken

A perfect winter warmer

Ingredients

¼	**Onion** (diced)
½	**Celery** stalk (sliced)
100g	**Potato** (diced)
1 tsp	**Butter**
1 tsp	**Plain Flour**
400ml	**Chicken Stock** (½ cube)
¼	**Lemon** (juice only)
1 sprig	**Tarragon** (large, chopped)
2 tbsp	**Double Cream**
100g	cooked **Chicken Breast** (shredded)

Preparation

1. Sauté the **onion**, **celery** and **potato** in 1 tsp **butter** for 5 mins, stirring to avoid browning.

2. Add the **flour** and stir for a few seconds before adding the **stock**. Simmer for 7 mins.

3. Stir in the **lemon juice** and **tarragon**.

4. Remove from the heat and blitz, before stirring in the **cream** and **chicken**.

5. Reheat, then serve garnished with some extra tarragon.

460 Cals

1 5-a-day

4g Fibre

13g SatFat

23g Fat

36g Protein

28g Carbs

Size
Medium
455g

Recipe Tip
Celery leaves are also edible and beneficial for health - try them in a stir fry!

Seafood Chowder

Like it fishy? Then you'll love this creamy concoction de la mer!

Ingredients

1	**Back Bacon** rasher (sliced)
¼	**Onion** (diced)
1 tsp	**Olive Oil**
1 tsp	**Plain Flour**
300ml	**Fish Stock** (½ cube)
50g	**Potato** (cubed)
100ml	**Milk** (semi-skimmed)
pinch	**Cayenne Pepper**
50g	**Cod** (sustainable, cubed)
50g	**Wild Salmon** (cubed)
40g	**Sweetcorn** (tinned)
100g	**Mussels** (cleaned)
1 tbsp	**Single Cream**
1 sprig	**Parsley** (chopped)

Preparation

1. Gently fry the **bacon** and **onion** in 1 tsp **oil** for 8 mins.

2. Stir in the **flour** and cook for 1 min. Add the **stock** and **potato**, and bring to the boil.

3. Pour in the **milk** with the **cayenne**, then place the **cod** and **salmon** into the mixture and cook for 3 mins.

4. Stir in the **sweetcorn** and **mussels**, and simmer for 3 mins more. Swirl through the **cream** and serve topped with **parsley**.

29g	44g	22g	7g	3g		1	480
Carbs	Protein	Fat	SatFat	Fibre		5-a-day	Cals

Recipe Tip

To reduce the environmental impact, use wild or organically farmed salmon

Size
Large
640g

5g Protein
2g Fat
0g SatFat
2g Fibre

Ciabatta
50g

26g Carbs
136 Cals
0 5-a-day

10g Protein
4g Fat
1g SatFat
3g Fibre

Ciabatta
100g

52g Carbs
271 Cals
0 5-a-day

2g Protein
2g Fat
1g Fibre

Croutons
15g

10g Carbs
66 Cals
0 5-a-day

4g Protein
4g Fat
1g Fibre

Croutons
30g

20g Carbs
132 Cals
0 5-a-day

5g Protein
2g Fat
0g SatFat
3g Fibre

Bread Roll (wholemeal)
50g

23g Carbs
122 Cals
0 5-a-day

8g Protein
2g Fat
1g SatFat
4g Fibre

Bread Roll (wholemeal)
75g

35g Carbs
183 Cals
0 5-a-day

Brie
25g

- 5g Protein
- 7g Fat
- 5g SatFat
- 0g Fibre
- 0g Carbs
- 86 Cals
- 0 5-a-day

Brie
50g

- 10g Protein
- 15g Fat
- 9g SatFat
- 0g Fibre
- 0g Carbs
- 172 Cals
- 0 5-a-day

Cheddar
25g

- 6g Protein
- 9g Fat
- 5g SatFat
- 0g Fibre
- 0g Carbs
- 104 Cals
- 0 5-a-day

Cheddar
50g

- 13g Protein
- 17g Fat
- 11g SatFat
- 0g Fibre
- 0g Carbs
- 208 Cals
- 0 5-a-day

Dolcelatte
25g

- 5g Protein
- 9g Fat
- 6g SatFat
- 0g Fibre
- 0g Carbs
- 99 Cals
- 0 5-a-day

Dolcelatte
50g

- 9g Protein
- 18g Fat
- 11g SatFat
- 0g Fibre
- 0g Carbs
- 197 Cals
- 0 5-a-day

4g Protein
5g Fat
3g SatFat
0g Fibre

Feta
25g

0g Carbs
63 Cals
0 5-a-day

8g Protein
10g Fat
7g SatFat
0g Fibre

Feta
50g

1g Carbs
125 Cals
0 5-a-day

5g Protein
6g Fat
4g SatFat
0g Fibre

Goat's Cheese
25g

0g Carbs
80 Cals
0 5-a-day

11g Protein
13g Fat
9g SatFat
0g Fibre

Goat's Cheese
50g

1g Carbs
160 Cals
0 5-a-day

7g Protein
8g Fat
5g SatFat
0g Fibre

Gruyère
25g

0g Carbs
102 Cals
0 5-a-day

14g Protein
17g Fat
10g SatFat
0g Fibre

Gruyère
50g

0g Carbs
205 Cals
0 5-a-day

6g Protein
6g Fat
4g SatFat
Halloumi
25g
0g Fibre
0g Carbs
78 Cals
0 5-a-day

12g Protein
12g Fat
8g SatFat
Halloumi
50g
0g Fibre
1g Carbs
157 Cals
0 5-a-day

4g Protein
3g Fat
2g SatFat
Parmesan
10g
0g Fibre
0g Carbs
42 Cals
0 5-a-day

7g Protein
6g Fat
4g SatFat
Parmesan
20g
0g Fibre
0g Carbs
83 Cals
0 5-a-day

6g Protein
9g Fat
6g SatFat
Stilton
25g
0g Fibre
0g Carbs
103 Cals
0 5-a-day

12g Protein
18g Fat
12g SatFat
Stilton
50g
0g Fibre
0g Carbs
205 Cals
0 5-a-day

27g
Protein

14g
Fat

6g
SatFat

Beef, Sirloin
100g, fried

0g
Fibre

0g
Carbs

233
Cals

0
5-a-day

54g
Protein

28g
Fat

12g
SatFat

Beef, Sirloin
200g, fried

0g
Fibre

0g
Carbs

466
Cals

0
5-a-day

4g
Protein

4g
Fat

1g
SatFat

Bacon
18g, grilled

0g
Fibre

0g
Carbs

52
Cals

0
5-a-day

8g
Protein

8g
Fat

3g
SatFat

Bacon
36g, grilled

0g
Fibre

0g
Carbs

103
Cals

0
5-a-day

32g
Protein

2g
Fat

1g
SatFat

Chicken Breast (no skin)
100g, grilled

0g
Fibre

0g
Carbs

148
Cals

0
5-a-day

64g
Protein

4g
Fat

1g
SatFat

Chicken Breast (no skin)
200g, grilled

0g
Fibre

0g
Carbs

296
Cals

0
5-a-day

Chorizo
25g

6g Protein
8g Fat
3g SatFat
0g Fibre
1g Carbs
99 Cals
0 5-a-day

Chorizo
50g

12g Protein
16g Fat
6g SatFat
1g Fibre
1g Carbs
198 Cals
0 5-a-day

Ham
100g, boiled

23g Protein
12g Fat
4g SatFat
0g Fibre
0g Carbs
204 Cals
0 5-a-day

Ham
200g, boiled

47g Protein
25g Fat
8g SatFat
0g Fibre
0g Carbs
408 Cals
0 5-a-day

Lamb Steak
100g, grilled

28g Protein
13g Fat
6g SatFat
0g Fibre
0g Carbs
231 Cals
0 5-a-day

Lamb Steak
200g, grilled

56g Protein
26g Fat
11g SatFat
0g Fibre
0g Carbs
462 Cals
0 5-a-day

8g Protein
6g Fat
2g SatFat
0g Fibre

Egg
60g, 1 egg, boiled

0g Carbs
86 Cals
0 5-a-day

17g Protein
12g Fat
3g SatFat
0g Fibre

Egg
120g, 2 eggs, boiled

0g Carbs
172 Cals
0 5-a-day

10g Protein
2g Fat
1g SatFat
5g Fibre

Quorn Chicken Pieces
75g

1g Carbs
72 Cals
0 5-a-day

21g Protein
4g Fat
2g SatFat
10g Fibre

Quorn Chicken Pieces
150g

2g Carbs
144 Cals
0 5-a-day

9g Protein
7g Fat
1g SatFat
1g Fibre

Tofu
40g, fried

1g Carbs
104 Cals
0 5-a-day

19g Protein
14g Fat
2g SatFat
1g Fibre

Tofu
80g, fried

2g Carbs
209 Cals
0 5-a-day

8g Protein

10g Fat

2g SatFat

Mackerel
40g, smoked

0g Fibre

0g Carbs

120 Cals

0 5-a-day

16g Protein

18g Fat

4g SatFat

Mackerel
75g, smoked

0g Fibre

0g Carbs

226 Cals

0 5-a-day

11g Protein

0g Fat

King Prawns
70g

0g Fibre

0g Carbs

48 Cals

0 5-a-day

16g Protein

0g Fat

King Prawns
100g

0g Fibre

0g Carbs

68 Cals

0 5-a-day

9g Protein

0g Fat

Crab (tinned in brine)
50g, drained

0g Fibre

0g Carbs

39 Cals

0 5-a-day

18g Protein

1g Fat

Crab (tinned in brine)
100g, drained

0g Fibre

0g Carbs

77 Cals

0 5-a-day

13g Protein
2g Fat
0g Fibre
3g Carbs
78 Cals
0 5-a-day

Mussels
75g

27g Protein
3g Fat
0g Fibre
5g Carbs
156 Cals
0 5-a-day

Mussels
150g

16g Protein
7g Fat
2g SatFat
0g Fibre
0g Carbs
129 Cals
0 5-a-day

Salmon
60g, baked

33g Protein
15g Fat
3g SatFat
0g Fibre
0g Carbs
269 Cals
0 5-a-day

Salmon
125g, baked

12g Protein
2g Fat
0g SatFat
0g Fibre
0g Carbs
65 Cals
0 5-a-day

Scallops
50g, fried

25g Protein
3g Fat
1g SatFat
0g Fibre
0g Carbs
130 Cals
0 5-a-day

Scallops
100g, fried

0g Protein

0g Fat

0g Fibre

Apple
40g, ¼ medium

5g Carbs | **20** Cals | **½** 5-a-day

0g Protein

0g Fat

1g Fibre

Apple
80g, ½ medium

9g Carbs | **41** Cals | **1** 5-a-day

0g Protein

0g Fat

0g Fibre

Lemon Peel
3g

0g Carbs | **1** Cals | **0** 5-a-day

0g Protein

0g Fat

1g Fibre

Lemon Peel
6g

1g Carbs | **3** Cals | **0** 5-a-day

0g Protein

0g Fat

1g Fibre

Pear
40g

4g Carbs | **17** Cals | **½** 5-a-day

0g Protein

0g Fat

2g Fibre

Pear
80g

9g Carbs | **34** Cals | **1** 5-a-day

Basil
6 leaves

0g Protein
0g Fat
0g Fibre
0g Carbs
1 Cals
0 5-a-day

Coriander
large sprig

0g Protein
0g Fat
0g Fibre
0g Carbs
1 Cals
0 5-a-day

Mint
5 leaves

0g Protein
0g Fat
0g Fibre
0g Carbs
1 Cals
0 5-a-day

Parsley
large sprig

0g Protein
0g Fat
0g Fibre
0g Carbs
1 Cals
0 5-a-day

Rosemary
sprig

0g Protein
0g Fat
0g Fibre
0g Carbs
1 Cals
0 5-a-day

Thyme
sprig

0g Protein
0g Fat
0g Fibre
0g Carbs
1 Cals
0 5-a-day

0g Protein
0g Fat
0g Fibre

Lemon Juice
15ml, 1 tbsp, ¼ lemon

0g Carbs | 1 Cals | 0 5-a-day

0g Protein
0g Fat
0g Fibre

Lemon Juice
30ml, 2 tbsp, ½ lemon

0g Carbs | 2 Cals | 0 5-a-day

0g Protein
0g Fat
0g Fibre

Lime Juice
10ml, ¼ lime

0g Carbs | 1 Cals | 0 5-a-day

0g Protein
0g Fat
0g Fibre

Lime Juice
20ml, ½ lime

0g Carbs | 2 Cals | 0 5-a-day

0g Protein
0g Fat
0g Fibre

Orange Juice (fresh)
15ml, 1 tbsp

1g Carbs | 5 Cals | 0 5-a-day

0g Protein
0g Fat
0g Fibre

Orange Juice (fresh)
30ml, 2 tbsp

2g Carbs | 10 Cals | 0 5-a-day

2g Protein			
6g Fat			
0g SatFat			
1g Fibre	1g Carbs	61 Cals	0 5-a-day

Almonds
10g, 1 tbsp

4g Protein			
11g Fat			
1g SatFat			
1g Fibre	1g Carbs	122 Cals	0 5-a-day

Almonds
20g, 2 tbsp

1g Protein			
7g Fat			
2g SatFat			
1g Fibre	0g Carbs	68 Cals	0 5-a-day

Brazil Nuts
10g, 1 tbsp

3g Protein			
14g Fat			
3g SatFat			
1g Fibre	1g Carbs	137 Cals	0 5-a-day

Brazil Nuts
20g, 2 tbsp

2g Protein			
5g Fat			
1g SatFat			
0g Fibre	2g Carbs	57 Cals	0 5-a-day

Cashews
10g, 1 tbsp

4g Protein			
10g Fat			
2g SatFat			
1g Fibre	4g Carbs	115 Cals	0 5-a-day

Cashews
20g, 2 tbsp

1g Protein

6g Fat

0g SatFat

1g Fibre

Hazelnuts
10g, 1 tbsp

1g Carbs | **65** Cals | **0** 5-a-day

3g Protein

13g Fat

1g SatFat

1g Fibre

Hazelnuts
20g, 2 tbsp

1g Carbs | **130** Cals | **0** 5-a-day

3g Protein

5g Fat

1g SatFat

1g Fibre

Peanuts
10g, 1 tbsp

1g Carbs | **56** Cals | **0** 5-a-day

5g Protein

9g Fat

2g SatFat

1g Fibre

Peanuts
20g, 2 tbsp

3g Carbs | **113** Cals | **0** 5-a-day

1g Protein

7g Fat

1g SatFat

1g Fibre

Pecans
10g, 1 tbsp

1g Carbs | **69** Cals | **0** 5-a-day

2g Protein

14g Fat

1g SatFat

1g Fibre

Pecans
20g, 2 tbsp

1g Carbs | **138** Cals | **0** 5-a-day

Pine Nuts
10g, 1 tbsp

- 1g Protein
- 7g Fat
- 0g SatFat
- 0g Fibre
- 0g Carbs
- 69 Cals
- 0 5-a-day

Pine Nuts
20g, 2 tbsp

- 3g Protein
- 14g Fat
- 1g SatFat
- 1g Fibre
- 1g Carbs
- 138 Cals
- 0 5-a-day

Pistachios
10g, 1 tbsp

- 2g Protein
- 6g Fat
- 1g SatFat
- 1g Fibre
- 1g Carbs
- 60 Cals
- 0 5-a-day

Pistachios
20g, 2 tbsp

- 4g Protein
- 11g Fat
- 1g SatFat
- 1g Fibre
- 2g Carbs
- 120 Cals
- 0 5-a-day

Walnuts
10g, 1 tbsp

- 1g Protein
- 7g Fat
- 1g SatFat
- 0g Fibre
- 0g Carbs
- 69 Cals
- 0 5-a-day

Walnuts
20g, 2 tbsp

- 3g Protein
- 14g Fat
- 2g SatFat
- 1g Fibre
- 1g Carbs
- 138 Cals
- 0 5-a-day

Pumpkin Seeds
10g, 1 tbsp

- 2g Protein
- 5g Fat
- 1g SatFat
- 1g Fibre
- 2g Carbs
- 57 Cals
- 0 5-a-day

Pumpkin Seeds
20g, 2 tbsp

- 5g Protein
- 9g Fat
- 1g SatFat
- 1g Fibre
- 3g Carbs
- 113 Cals
- 0 5-a-day

Sesame Seeds
3g, ½ tsp

- 1g Protein
- 2g Fat
- 0g SatFat
- 0g Fibre
- 0g Carbs
- 18 Cals
- 0 5-a-day

Sesame Seeds
5g, 1 tsp

- 1g Protein
- 3g Fat
- 1g SatFat
- 1g Fibre
- 0g Carbs
- 30 Cals
- 0 5-a-day

Sunflower Seeds
10g, 1 tbsp

- 2g Protein
- 5g Fat
- 1g SatFat
- 1g Fibre
- 2g Carbs
- 58 Cals
- 0 5-a-day

Sunflower Seeds
20g, 2 tbsp

- 4g Protein
- 10g Fat
- 1g SatFat
- 2g Fibre
- 4g Carbs
- 115 Cals
- 0 5-a-day

Basmati Rice *(cooked)*
100g

- 3g Protein
- 1g Fat
- 1g Fibre
- 27g Carbs
- 117 Cals
- 0 5-a-day

Basmati Rice *(cooked)*
200g

- 6g Protein
- 1g Fat
- 1g Fibre
- 53g Carbs
- 234 Cals
- 0 5-a-day

Brown Rice *(cooked)*
100g

- 4g Protein
- 1g Fat
- 2g Fibre
- 29g Carbs
- 132 Cals
- 0 5-a-day

Brown Rice *(cooked)*
200g

- 7g Protein
- 2g Fat
- 3g Fibre
- 58g Carbs
- 264 Cals
- 0 5-a-day

Wild Rice *(cooked)*
100g

- 5g Protein
- 1g Fat
- 3g Fibre
- 32g Carbs
- 145 Cals
- 0 5-a-day

Wild Rice *(cooked)*
200g

- 11g Protein
- 1g Fat
- 5g Fibre
- 63g Carbs
- 290 Cals
- 0 5-a-day

6g Protein

1g Fat

3g Fibre

Egg Noodles (cooked)
100g

36g Carbs **166** Cals **0** 5-a-day

12g Protein

2g Fat

6g Fibre

Egg Noodles (cooked)
200g

71g Carbs **332** Cals **0** 5-a-day

5g Protein

0g Fat

3g Fibre

Pasta (cooked)
100g

33g Carbs **146** Cals **0** 5-a-day

10g Protein

1g Fat

5g Fibre

Pasta (cooked)
200g

66g Carbs **292** Cals **0** 5-a-day

5g Protein

1g Fat

4g Fibre

Pasta, Wholewheat (cooked)
100g

28g Carbs **134** Cals **0** 5-a-day

10g Protein

2g Fat

8g Fibre

Pasta, Wholewheat (cooked)
200g

55g Carbs **268** Cals **0** 5-a-day

Pasta, Orzo (cooked)
100g

- 5g Protein
- 1g Fat
- 1g Fibre
- 32g Carbs
- 160 Cals
- 0 5-a-day

Pasta, Orzo (cooked)
200g

- 10g Protein
- 1g Fat
- 2g Fibre
- 64g Carbs
- 320 Cals
- 0 5-a-day

Rice Noodles (cooked)
100g

- 2g Protein
- 0g Fat
- 1g Fibre
- 28g Carbs
- 123 Cals
- 0 5-a-day

Rice Noodles (cooked)
200g

- 3g Protein
- 0g Fat
- 1g Fibre
- 56g Carbs
- 246 Cals
- 0 5-a-day

Bulgur Wheat (cooked)
80g

- 2g Protein
- 0g Fat
- 7g Fibre
- 16g Carbs
- 75 Cals
- 0 5-a-day

Bulgur Wheat (cooked)
160g

- 4g Protein
- 1g Fat
- 14g Fibre
- 32g Carbs
- 150 Cals
- 0 5-a-day

6g Protein

Couscous (cooked)
80g

1g Fat

2g Fibre | **30g** Carbs | **142** Cals | **0** 5-a-day

12g Protein

Couscous (cooked)
160g

2g Fat

4g Fibre | **60g** Carbs | **285** Cals | **0** 5-a-day

2g Protein

Pearl Barley (cooked)
80g

0g Fat

3g Fibre | **22g** Carbs | **96** Cals | **0** 5-a-day

4g Protein

Pearl Barley (cooked)
160g

1g Fat

6g Fibre | **44g** Carbs | **192** Cals | **0** 5-a-day

4g Protein

Quinoa (cooked)
80g

2g Fat

2g Fibre | **15g** Carbs | **92** Cals | **0** 5-a-day

7g Protein

Quinoa (cooked)
160g

3g Fat

5g Fibre | **30g** Carbs | **184** Cals | **0** 5-a-day

Asparagus Tips
40g

1g Protein	0g Fat	1g Fibre

1g Carbs | 10 Cals | ½ 5-a-day

Asparagus Tips
80g

2g Protein	0g Fat	2g Fibre

2g Carbs | 20 Cals | 1 5-a-day

Artichokes (tinned)
40g, drained

1g Protein	0g Fat	1g Fibre

2g Carbs | 11 Cals | ½ 5-a-day

Artichokes (tinned)
80g, drained

1g Protein	0g Fat	1g Fibre

4g Carbs | 23 Cals | 1 5-a-day

Aubergine
40g

0g Protein	0g Fat	1g Fibre

1g Carbs | 6 Cals | ½ 5-a-day

Aubergine
80g

1g Protein	0g Fat	2g Fibre

2g Carbs | 12 Cals | 1 5-a-day

Avocado
35g

1g Protein
7g Fat
1g SatFat
2g Fibre
1g Carbs
67 Cals
0 5-a-day

Avocado
70g

1g Protein
14g Fat
3g SatFat
3g Fibre
1g Carbs
133 Cals
½ 5-a-day

Bamboo Shoots
40g

1g Protein
0g Fat
1g Fibre
0g Carbs
4 Cals
½ 5-a-day

Bamboo Shoots
80g

1g Protein
0g Fat
2g Fibre
1g Carbs
9 Cals
1 5-a-day

Beansprouts
40g

1g Protein
0g Fat
1g Fibre
2g Carbs
12 Cals
½ 5-a-day

Beansprouts
80g

2g Protein
0g Fat
2g Fibre
3g Carbs
25 Cals
1 5-a-day

1g
Protein

0g
Fat

1g
Fibre

Beetroot
40g, ½ medium, peeled

3g
Carbs

14
Cals

½
5-a-day

1g
Protein

0g
Fat

2g
Fibre

Beetroot
80g, peeled

6g
Carbs

29
Cals

1
5-a-day

3g
Protein

0g
Fat

2g
Fibre

Black Eye Beans (tinned)
40g, drained

7g
Carbs

46
Cals

½
5-a-day

6g
Protein

0g
Fat

4g
Fibre

Black Eye Beans (tinned)
80g, drained

14g
Carbs

91
Cals

1
5-a-day

2g
Protein

0g
Fat

3g
Fibre

Broad Beans
40g, boiled

2g
Carbs

19
Cals

½
5-a-day

4g
Protein

1g
Fat

6g
Fibre

Broad Beans
80g, boiled

4g
Carbs

38
Cals

1
5-a-day

2g Protein

0g Fat

2g Fibre

Broccoli
40g

1g Carbs | **14** Cals | **½** 5-a-day

3g Protein

0g Fat

3g Fibre

Broccoli
80g

3g Carbs | **27** Cals | **1** 5-a-day

2g Protein

0g Fat

2g Fibre

Butter Beans (tinned)
40g, drained

5g Carbs | **31** Cals | **½** 5-a-day

5g Protein

0g Fat

5g Fibre

Butter Beans (tinned)
80g, drained

10g Carbs | **62** Cals | **1** 5-a-day

0g Protein

0g Fat

1g Fibre

Butternut Squash
40g

3g Carbs | **14** Cals | **½** 5-a-day

1g Protein

0g Fat

2g Fibre

Butternut Squash
80g

7g Carbs | **29** Cals | **1** 5-a-day

Cabbage
20g

0g Protein
0g Fat
1g Fibre
1g Carbs
5 Cals
0 5-a-day

Cabbage
40g

1g Protein
0g Fat
2g Fibre
2g Carbs
11 Cals
½ 5-a-day

Cabbage, Red
20g

0g Protein
0g Fat
1g Fibre
1g Carbs
4 Cals
0 5-a-day

Cabbage, Red
40g

0g Protein
0g Fat
1g Fibre
1g Carbs
8 Cals
½ 5-a-day

Cannellini Beans (tinned)
40g, drained

3g Protein
0g Fat
2g Fibre
6g Carbs
38 Cals
½ 5-a-day

Cannellini Beans (tinned)
80g, drained

6g Protein
0g Fat
5g Fibre
12g Carbs
75 Cals
1 5-a-day

Capers
10g, 1 tbsp

0g Protein
0g Fat
0g Fibre
0g Carbs
3 Cals
0 5-a-day

Capers
20g, 2 tbsp

0g Protein
0g Fat
1g Fibre
1g Carbs
6 Cals
0 5-a-day

Carrot
40g, ½ medium

0g Protein
0g Fat
2g Fibre
3g Carbs
14 Cals
½ 5-a-day

Carrot
80g, 1 medium

0g Protein
0g Fat
3g Fibre
6g Carbs
27 Cals
1 5-a-day

Cauliflower
40g

1g Protein
0g Fat
1g Fibre
2g Carbs
12 Cals
½ 5-a-day

Cauliflower
80g

2g Protein
0g Fat
1g Fibre
4g Carbs
24 Cals
1 5-a-day

Celery 40g

0g Protein
0g Fat
1g Fibre
0g Carbs
3 Cals
½ 5-a-day

Celery 80g

0g Protein
0g Fat
1g Fibre
1g Carbs
6 Cals
1 5-a-day

Chestnuts 40g

2g Protein
1g Fat
2g Fibre
13g Carbs
70 Cals
½ 5-a-day

Chestnuts 80g

3g Protein
1g Fat
5g Fibre
27g Carbs
141 Cals
1 5-a-day

Chickpeas (tinned) 40g, drained

3g Protein
1g Fat
2g Fibre
6g Carbs
46 Cals
½ 5-a-day

Chickpeas (tinned) 80g, drained

6g Protein
2g Fat
4g Fibre
13g Carbs
92 Cals
1 5-a-day

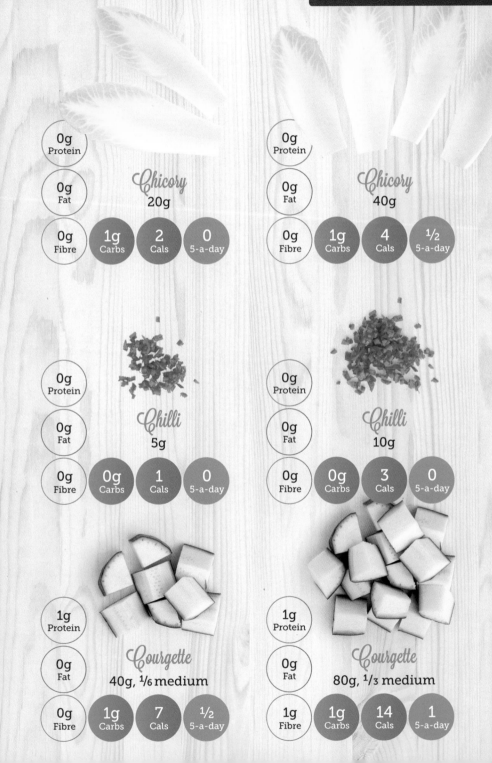

Chicory
20g

0g Protein
0g Fat
0g Fibre
1g Carbs
2 Cals
0 5-a-day

Chicory
40g

0g Protein
0g Fat
0g Fibre
1g Carbs
4 Cals
½ 5-a-day

Chilli
5g

0g Protein
0g Fat
0g Fibre
0g Carbs
1 Cals
0 5-a-day

Chilli
10g

0g Protein
0g Fat
0g Fibre
0g Carbs
3 Cals
0 5-a-day

Courgette
40g, ⅙ medium

1g Protein
0g Fat
0g Fibre
1g Carbs
7 Cals
½ 5-a-day

Courgette
80g, ⅓ medium

1g Protein
0g Fat
1g Fibre
1g Carbs
14 Cals
1 5-a-day

Cucumber
40g, ⅛ medium

0g Protein	0g Fat	0g Fibre	0g Carbs	6 Cals	½ 5-a-day

Cucumber
80g, ¼ medium

1g Protein	0g Fat	1g Fibre	1g Carbs	11 Cals	1 5-a-day

Fennel
40g

0g Protein	0g Fat	1g Fibre	1g Carbs	5 Cals	½ 5-a-day

Fennel
80g

1g Protein	0g Fat	3g Fibre	1g Carbs	10 Cals	1 5-a-day

Garlic
3g

0g Protein	0g Fat	0g Fibre	0g Carbs	3 Cals	0 5-a-day

Garlic
6g

1g Protein	0g Fat	0g Fibre	1g Carbs	6 Cals	0 5-a-day

Ginger
5g, 1 inch, peeled

0g Protein
0g Fat
0g Fibre
0g Carbs
2 Cals
0 5-a-day

Ginger
10g, 2 inches, peeled

0g Protein
0g Fat
0g Fibre
1g Carbs
4 Cals
0 5-a-day

Green Beans
40g

1g Protein
0g Fat
1g Fibre
1g Carbs
10 Cals
½ 5-a-day

Green Beans
80g

2g Protein
0g Fat
3g Fibre
2g Carbs
19 Cals
1 5-a-day

Kale
20g, handful

1g Protein
0g Fat
1g Fibre
0g Carbs
7 Cals
0 5-a-day

Kale
40g, 2 handfuls

1g Protein
1g Fat
2g Fibre
1g Carbs
13 Cals
½ 5-a-day

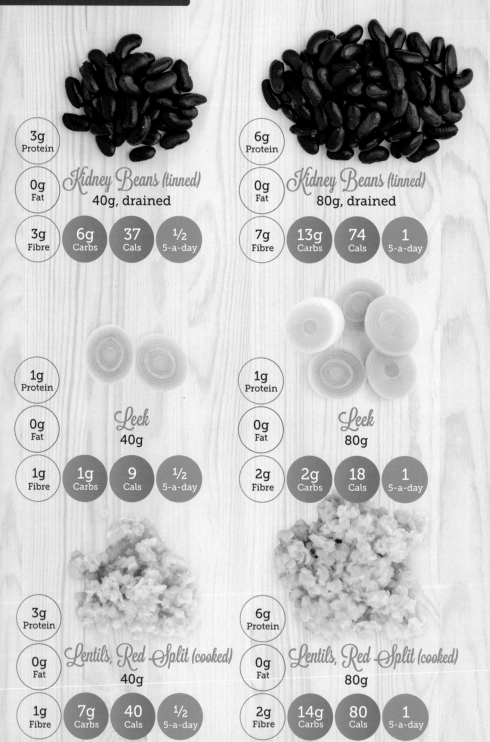

3g Protein

0g Fat

3g Fibre

Kidney Beans (tinned)
40g, drained

6g Carbs **37** Cals **½** 5-a-day

6g Protein

0g Fat

7g Fibre

Kidney Beans (tinned)
80g, drained

13g Carbs **74** Cals **1** 5-a-day

1g Protein

0g Fat

1g Fibre

Leek
40g

1g Carbs **9** Cals **½** 5-a-day

1g Protein

0g Fat

2g Fibre

Leek
80g

2g Carbs **18** Cals **1** 5-a-day

3g Protein

0g Fat

1g Fibre

Lentils, Red Split (cooked)
40g

7g Carbs **40** Cals **½** 5-a-day

6g Protein

0g Fat

2g Fibre

Lentils, Red Split (cooked)
80g

14g Carbs **80** Cals **1** 5-a-day

3g Protein

0g Fat

1g Fibre

Lentils (tinned)
40g, drained

7g Carbs | **41** Cals | **½** 5-a-day

7g Protein

0g Fat

3g Fibre

Lentils (tinned)
80g, drained

14g Carbs | **82** Cals | **1** 5-a-day

1g Protein

0g Fat

1g Fibre

Mangetout
40g

2g Carbs | **13** Cals | **½** 5-a-day

3g Protein

0g Fat

2g Fibre

Mangetout
80g

3g Carbs | **26** Cals | **1** 5-a-day

3g Protein

0g Fat

2g Fibre

Mixed Beans (tinned)
40g, drained

5g Carbs | **39** Cals | **½** 5-a-day

5g Protein

1g Fat

5g Fibre

Mixed Beans (tinned)
80g, drained

10g Carbs | **78** Cals | **1** 5-a-day

1g Protein			
0g Fat			
2g Fibre	1g Carbs	12 Cals	½ 5-a-day

Okra
40g

2g Protein			
1g Fat			
4g Fibre	2g Carbs	25 Cals	1 5-a-day

Okra
80g

0g Protein			
0g Fat			
0g Fibre	0g Carbs	3 Cals	½ 5-a-day

Mushrooms
40g

1g Protein			
0g Fat			
1g Fibre	0g Carbs	6 Cals	1 5-a-day

Mushrooms
80g

2g Protein			
0g Fat			
2g Fibre	15g Carbs	68 Cals	0 5-a-day

New Potatoes
100g, boiled

4g Protein			
0g Fat			
4g Fibre	30g Carbs	136 Cals	0 5-a-day

New Potatoes
200g, boiled

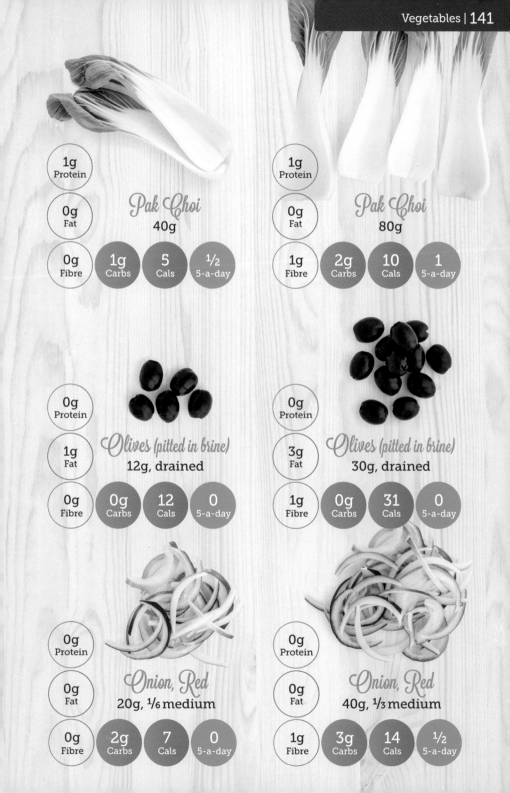

Pak Choi
40g

- 1g Protein
- 0g Fat
- 0g Fibre
- 1g Carbs
- 5 Cals
- ½ 5-a-day

Pak Choi
80g

- 1g Protein
- 0g Fat
- 1g Fibre
- 2g Carbs
- 10 Cals
- 1 5-a-day

Olives (pitted in brine)
12g, drained

- 0g Protein
- 1g Fat
- 0g Fibre
- 0g Carbs
- 12 Cals
- 0 5-a-day

Olives (pitted in brine)
30g, drained

- 0g Protein
- 3g Fat
- 1g Fibre
- 0g Carbs
- 31 Cals
- 0 5-a-day

Onion, Red
20g, ⅙ medium

- 0g Protein
- 0g Fat
- 0g Fibre
- 2g Carbs
- 7 Cals
- 0 5-a-day

Onion, Red
40g, ⅓ medium

- 0g Protein
- 0g Fat
- 1g Fibre
- 3g Carbs
- 14 Cals
- ½ 5-a-day

1g Protein

0g Fat

2g Fibre

Parsnip
40g

5g Carbs · **26** Cals · **½** 5-a-day

1g Protein

1g Fat

4g Fibre

Parsnip
80g

10g Carbs · **51** Cals · **1** 5-a-day

3g Protein

1g Fat

2g Fibre

Peas
40g

4g Carbs · **32** Cals · **½** 5-a-day

5g Protein

1g Fat

4g Fibre

Peas
80g

8g Carbs · **63** Cals · **1** 5-a-day

3g Protein

0g Fat

1g Fibre

Peas, Split Green (cooked)
40g

9g Carbs · **50** Cals · **½** 5-a-day

7g Protein

1g Fat

3g Fibre

Peas, Split Green (cooked)
80g

18g Carbs · **101** Cals · **1** 5-a-day

Rocket
20g, handful

1g Protein
0g Fat
0g Fibre
0g Carbs
4 Cals
0 5-a-day

Rocket
40g, 2 handfuls

1g Protein
0g Fat
1g Fibre
0g Carbs
7 Cals
½ 5-a-day

Pepper
40g, ¼ small

0g Protein
0g Fat
1g Fibre
2g Carbs
9 Cals
½ 5-a-day

Pepper
80g, ½ small

1g Protein
0g Fat
2g Fibre
4g Carbs
18 Cals
1 5-a-day

Soya Beans
40g

6g Protein
3g Fat
0g SatFat
3g Fibre
2g Carbs
56 Cals
½ 5-a-day

Soya Beans
80g

11g Protein
6g Fat
1g SatFat
6g Fibre
4g Carbs
113 Cals
1 5-a-day

1g
Protein

0g
Fat

Spinach
20g, handful

1g
Fibre

0g
Carbs

5
Cals

0
5-a-day

1g
Protein

0g
Fat

Spinach
40g, 2 handfuls

1g
Fibre

1g
Carbs

10
Cals

½
5-a-day

0g
Protein

0g
Fat

Spring Onion
20g

0g
Fibre

1g
Carbs

5
Cals

0
5-a-day

1g
Protein

0g
Fat

Spring Onion
40g

1g
Fibre

1g
Carbs

9
Cals

½
5-a-day

1g
Protein

0g
Fat

Sugar Snap Peas
40g

1g
Fibre

2g
Carbs

14
Cals

½
5-a-day

3g
Protein

0g
Fat

Sugar Snap Peas
80g

2g
Fibre

4g
Carbs

27
Cals

1
5-a-day

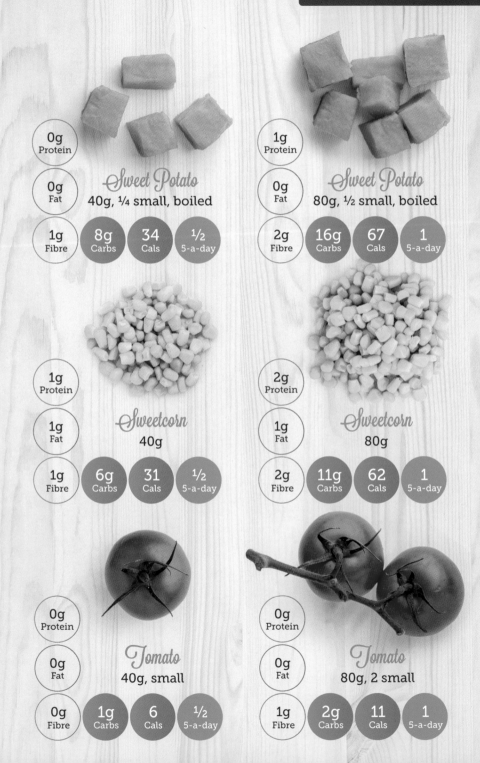

Sweet Potato
40g, ¼ small, boiled

0g Protein
0g Fat
1g Fibre
8g Carbs
34 Cals
½ 5-a-day

Sweet Potato
80g, ½ small, boiled

1g Protein
0g Fat
2g Fibre
16g Carbs
67 Cals
1 5-a-day

Sweetcorn
40g

1g Protein
1g Fat
1g Fibre
6g Carbs
31 Cals
½ 5-a-day

Sweetcorn
80g

2g Protein
1g Fat
2g Fibre
11g Carbs
62 Cals
1 5-a-day

Tomato
40g, small

0g Protein
0g Fat
0g Fibre
1g Carbs
6 Cals
½ 5-a-day

Tomato
80g, 2 small

0g Protein
0g Fat
1g Fibre
2g Carbs
11 Cals
1 5-a-day

0g Protein			
0g Fat	*Tomatoes, Cherry* 40g, 4 small		
1g Fibre	1g Carbs	9 Cals	½ 5-a-day

1g Protein			
0g Fat	*Tomatoes, Cherry* 80g, 8 small		
1g Fibre	3g Carbs	18 Cals	1 5-a-day

1g Protein			
2g Fat			
0g SatFat	*Tomato, Sun-dried (in oil)* 20g, drained		
1g Fibre	2g Carbs	35 Cals	0 5-a-day

2g Protein			
5g Fat			
1g SatFat	*Tomato, Sun-dried (in oil)* 40g, drained		
3g Fibre	3g Carbs	69 Cals	0 5-a-day

1g Protein			
0g Fat	*Watercress* 20g, large handful		
0g Fibre	0g Carbs	4 Cals	0 5-a-day

1g Protein			
0g Fat	*Watercress* 40g, 2 large handfuls		
1g Fibre	0g Carbs	9 Cals	½ 5-a-day

Balsamic Vinegar
5ml, 1 tsp

- 0g Protein
- 0g Fat
- 0g Fibre
- 2g Carbs
- 8 Cals
- 0 5-a-day

Balsamic Vinegar
15ml, 1 tbsp

- 0g Protein
- 0g Fat
- 0g Fibre
- 6g Carbs
- 24 Cals
- 0 5-a-day

Butter
5g, 1 tsp

- 0g Protein
- 4g Fat
- 3g SatFat
- 0g Fibre
- 0g Carbs
- 37 Cals
- 0 5-a-day

Butter
15g, 1 tbsp

- 0g Protein
- 12g Fat
- 8g SatFat
- 0g Fibre
- 0g Carbs
- 112 Cals
- 0 5-a-day

Chilli Oil
4g, 1 tsp

- 0g Protein
- 4g Fat
- 1g SatFat
- 0g Fibre
- 0g Carbs
- 36 Cals
- 0 5-a-day

Chilli Oil
12g, 1 tbsp

- 0g Protein
- 12g Fat
- 2g SatFat
- 0g Fibre
- 0g Carbs
- 108 Cals
- 0 5-a-day

Coconut Milk (tinned)
100ml

1g Protein
17g Fat
15g SatFat
0g Fibre
3g Carbs
169 Cals
0 5-a-day

Coconut Milk (tinned)
200ml

2g Protein
34g Fat
29g SatFat
1g Fibre
7g Carbs
338 Cals
0 5-a-day

Cornflour
15g

0g Protein
0g Fat
0g Fibre
14g Carbs
53 Cals
0 5-a-day

Cornflour
30g

0g Protein
0g Fat
0g Fibre
28g Carbs
106 Cals
0 5-a-day

Fish Sauce
5ml, 1 tsp

0g Protein
0g Fat
0g Fibre
0g Carbs
4 Cals
0 5-a-day

Fish Sauce
15ml, 1 tbsp

1g Protein
0g Fat
0g Fibre
1g Carbs
11 Cals
0 5-a-day

Flour (plain)
15g

1g Protein
0g Fat
1g Fibre
12g Carbs
53 Cals
0 5-a-day

Flour (plain)
30g

3g Protein
0g Fat
1g Fibre
24g Carbs
106 Cals
0 5-a-day

Honey
6g, 1 tsp

0g Protein
0g Fat
0g Fibre
5g Carbs
17 Cals
0 5-a-day

Honey
18g, 1 tbsp

0g Protein
0g Fat
0g Fibre
14g Carbs
52 Cals
0 5-a-day

Horseradish Sauce
5g, 1 tsp

0g Protein
1g Fat
0g Fibre
1g Carbs
14 Cals
0 5-a-day

Horseradish Sauce
15g, 1 tbsp

0g Protein
3g Fat
0g Fibre
3g Carbs
42 Cals
0 5-a-day

Maple Syrup
6g, 1 tsp

0g Protein
0g Fat
0g Fibre
4g Carbs
16 Cals
0 5-a-day

Maple Syrup
17g, 1 tbsp

0g Protein
0g Fat
0g Fibre
11g Carbs
45 Cals
0 5-a-day

Mirin
5ml, 1 tsp

0g Protein
0g Fat
0g Fibre
3g Carbs
15 Cals
0 5-a-day

Mirin
15ml, 1 tbsp

0g Protein
0g Fat
0g Fibre
8g Carbs
45 Cals
0 5-a-day

Mustard, Dijon
5g, 1 tsp

0g Protein
1g Fat
0g Fibre
0g Carbs
8 Cals
0 5-a-day

Mustard, Dijon
15g, 1 tbsp

1g Protein
2g Fat
0g Fibre
1g Carbs
23 Cals
0 5-a-day

Mustard, English
5g, 1 tsp

0g Protein
0g Fat
0g Fibre
0g Carbs
7 Cals
0 5-a-day

Mustard, English
15g, 1 tbsp

1g Protein
1g Fat
0g Fibre
1g Carbs
21 Cals
0 5-a-day

Mustard, Wholegrain
5g, 1 tsp

0g Protein
1g Fat
0g Fibre
0g Carbs
7 Cals
0 5-a-day

Mustard, Wholegrain
15g, 1 tbsp

1g Protein
2g Fat
1g Fibre
1g Carbs
21 Cals
0 5-a-day

Olive Oil
4g, 1 tsp

0g Protein
4g Fat
1g SatFat
0g Fibre
0g Carbs
36 Cals
0 5-a-day

Olive Oil
12g, 1 tbsp

0g Protein
12g Fat
2g SatFat
0g Fibre
0g Carbs
108 Cals
0 5-a-day

1g
Protein

6g
Fat

1g
SatFat

0g
Fibre

Pesto
15g, 1 tbsp

1g
Carbs

63
Cals

0
5-a-day

2g
Protein

13g
Fat

2g
SatFat

0g
Fibre

Pesto
30g, 2 tbsp

1g
Carbs

126
Cals

0
5-a-day

0g
Protein

0g
Fat

0g
Fibre

Red Wine Vinegar
5ml, 1 tsp

0g
Carbs

1
Cals

0
5-a-day

0g
Protein

0g
Fat

0g
Fibre

Red Wine Vinegar
15ml, 1 tbsp

0g
Carbs

3
Cals

0
5-a-day

0g
Protein

0g
Fat

0g
Fibre

Rice Wine Vinegar
5ml, 1 tsp

0g
Carbs

1
Cals

0
5-a-day

0g
Protein

0g
Fat

0g
Fibre

Rice Wine Vinegar
15ml, 1 tbsp

0g
Carbs

3
Cals

0
5-a-day

Satay Sauce
5g, 1 tsp

0g Protein
1g Fat
0g Fibre
1g Carbs
10 Cals
0 5-a-day

Satay Sauce
15g, 1 tbsp

1g Protein
2g Fat
0g Fibre
2g Carbs
29 Cals
0 5-a-day

Sesame Oil
4g, 1 tsp

0g Protein
4g Fat
1g SatFat
0g Fibre
0g Carbs
36 Cals
0 5-a-day

Sesame Oil
12g, 1 tbsp

0g Protein
12g Fat
2g SatFat
0g Fibre
0g Carbs
108 Cals
0 5-a-day

Soy Sauce
5ml, 1 tsp

0g Protein
0g Fat
0g Fibre
1g Carbs
4 Cals
0 5-a-day

Soy Sauce
15ml, 1 tbsp

0g Protein
0g Fat
0g Fibre
3g Carbs
12 Cals
0 5-a-day

Tahini
5g, 1 tsp

1g Protein
3g Fat
0g SatFat
1g Fibre
0g Carbs
33 Cals
0 5-a-day

Tahini
15g, 1 tbsp

3g Protein
9g Fat
1g SatFat
1g Fibre
1g Carbs
99 Cals
0 5-a-day

Tomato Purée
15g, 1 tbsp

1g Protein
0g Fat
1g Fibre
2g Carbs
10 Cals
0 5-a-day

Tomato Purée
30g, 2 tbsp

1g Protein
0g Fat
1g Fibre
4g Carbs
20 Cals
0 5-a-day

White Wine Vinegar
5ml, 1 tsp

0g Protein
0g Fat
0g Fibre
0g Carbs
1 Cals
0 5-a-day

White Wine Vinegar
15ml, 1 tbsp

0g Protein
0g Fat
0g Fibre
0g Carbs
3 Cals
0 5-a-day

Crème Fraîche (half fat)
15g, 1 tbsp

- 0g Protein
- 2g Fat
- 2g SatFat
- 0g Fibre
- 1g Carbs
- 24 Cals
- 0 5-a-day

Crème Fraîche (half fat)
30g, 2 tbsp

- 1g Protein
- 5g Fat
- 3g SatFat
- 0g Fibre
- 1g Carbs
- 49 Cals
- 0 5-a-day

Natural Yogurt (fat free)
15g, 1 tbsp

- 1g Protein
- 0g Fat
- 0g Fibre
- 1g Carbs
- 8 Cals
- 0 5-a-day

Natural Yogurt (fat free)
30g, 2 tbsp

- 2g Protein
- 0g Fat
- 0g Fibre
- 2g Carbs
- 16 Cals
- 0 5-a-day

Soured Cream
15g, 1 tbsp

- 0g Protein
- 3g Fat
- 2g SatFat
- 0g Fibre
- 1g Carbs
- 31 Cals
- 0 5-a-day

Soured Cream
30g, 2 tbsp

- 1g Protein
- 6g Fat
- 4g SatFat
- 0g Fibre
- 1g Carbs
- 62 Cals
- 0 5-a-day

Soup Index

Ingredients

About the Authors

Chris Cheyette BSc (Hons) MSc RD
Diabetes Specialist Dietitian

Chris is a Diabetes Specialist Dietitian within the NHS, working with people with type 1, type 2 and gestational diabetes. Chris has spearheaded a number of projects over the years, many with the aim of improving diabetes educational resources. These include an educational DVD for young people with diabetes, which earned him the 2007 British Dietetic Association Elizabeth Washington Award. Chris has also published a number of journal articles on weight management and diabetes. He regularly undertakes local and national presentations to healthcare professionals, has done TV & newspaper interviews, and has participated as a guest expert in online discussions.

Yello Balolia BA (Hons)
Entrepreneur & Creative Photographer

Having achieved a first class honours degree in Photography, Canada-born, Blackpool-bred and now London-based Yello used his entrepreneurial and creative skills to found Chello Publishing Limited with Chris Cheyette, to publish Carbs & Cals (**www.carbsandcals.com**), the bestselling and multi-award-winning book and app for diabetes and weight management. He has also undertaken a series of creative projects including private commissions (**www.yellobalolia.com**) and, as a keen musician, Yello recently set up Ukulology - a visual and effective way of learning the ukulele (**www.ukulology.com**).

Awards

WINNER
Category: **Best Dietary Management Initiative**
Quality in Care Programme 2014

Carbs & Cals won **Best Dietary Management Initiative** at the Quality in Care Awards 2014

The Carbs & Cals App won **New Product of the Year** in the Complete Nutrition Awards 2012

Winner of the 2011 Dame Barbara Clayton Award

Carbs & Cals won the BDA Dame Barbara Clayton **Award for Innovation & Excellence** 2011

Carbs & Cals APP
WINNER
NEW PRODUCT OF THE YEAR

Carbs & Cals